WANTING TO *Live*

Overcoming the Seduction of Suicide

ALSO BY NEROLI DUFFY

Wanting to Be Born: The Cry of the Soul

ALSO BY MARILYN BARRICK

Sacred Psychology of Love:
The Quest for Relationships that Unite Heart and Soul

Sacred Psychology of Change:
Life as a Voyage of Transformation

Dreams: Exploring the Secrets of Your Soul

Emotions: Transforming Anger, Fear and Pain

Soul Reflections: Many Lives, Many Journeys

WANTING TO *Live*

Overcoming the Seduction of Suicide

Dr. Neroli Duffy and Marilyn C. Barrick, Ph.D.

SUMMIT UNIVERSITY PRESS®
Corwin Springs, Montana

WANTING TO LIVE: OVERCOMING THE SEDUCTION OF SUICIDE
by Dr. Neroli Duffy and Marilyn C. Barrick, Ph.D.
based on teachings of Elizabeth Clare Prophet
 For information, please contact Summit University Press, PO Box 5000, Corwin Springs, MT 59030-5000 USA. Tel: 1-800-245-5445 or 406-848-9500
Web site: www.summituniversitypress.com
E-mail: info@summituniversitypress.com

Library of Congress Control Number: 2003115260
ISBN: 0-922729-92-1

SUMMIT UNIVERSITY PRESS®

Cover photograph: John Beale

Printed in the United States of America

07 06 05 04 6 5 4 3 2 1

To the many souls who exit life on earth
through despondency, and yet
who really want to live.

IMPORTANT NOTICE

This book is intended to provide general spiritual insight and should not be used as a substitute for professional counseling and other forms of intervention.

If you are considering suicide, or if someone you know has exhibited any of the warning signs of suicide, professional help should be sought immediately.

Contents

Foreword

A Way Out—Or a Way Back?

Blackness upon blackness. That was all Joan could think about. There was no point to getting up in the morning, no point to bathing, no point to looking outside. There was no point to anything ... simply blackness.

The only glimmer of caring in Joan's life was her ten-year-old daughter, Susan. Susan competed on horseback. Susan needed her. But today even Susan was fading into blackness.

Joan rummaged through the pile of junk on the bathroom counter and found the amber bottle of sleeping pills. "Susan has a competition today," went through her head into blackness. She almost felt something beyond her move her arms. Joan poured the pills into her hand.

* * *

If Joan chooses to exit from life, where will her choice take her? In this unique and inspiring book, a leading new age spiritual teacher, a medical doctor and a clinical psychologist part the veil for a startling look beyond the physical world into a realm we don't usually see: malignant spirits coaxing depressed but beautiful people into suicide; a bleak, painful existence in a dark, frightening level of consciousness; and lost souls immediately coming back into a new lifetime to face the same test all over again.

Most important, *Wanting to Live* offers powerful, life-changing partnerships with heavenly rescuers, practical tools and priceless insights for suicidal people and their loved ones to allow light to transform a dark world.

Hope in a life of hopelessness—this book will save many lives.

LOIS DRAKE

The Gift of Life

Life is a priceless gift—yet every year, thousands of despondent souls end their own lives. Many are children and teenagers who assume they are leaving all their troubles behind them as they go to a better world.

Everybody really wants *life,* even when they end it. Yet why are so many dying to live?

An understanding of who we are and the spiritual laws that govern our existence can help people in their darkest moments when they are choosing between life and death—unable, it seems, to tell the difference—while heaven itself awaits their fate.

PART 1

UNDERSTANDING SUICIDE

A Special Place in God's Plan

Each of us has our own special place in God's plan. We came into embodiment to take our place on the stage of life and to offer the unique gift that only we can give.

We all have a special mission to perform in life. It may be to give birth to our children, to publish a book, to offer our gift of drama or engineering or music or science—a mission that only we can complete.

Those who undergo a near-death experience often report being told of their mission at "life reviews" with angels and masters of light. In fact, at the conclusion of a life on earth, each of us takes stock of the life we have lived. We review our mission—what we have made of the opportunity of life. And we see the consequences of our actions—both good and bad. The successes and failures are all seen as learning experiences.

Those who return from a near-death experience often do so because they have a specific mission they have not yet fulfilled. They return with a real sense of purpose, seeking to finish what they came to earth to do.

There is a vast difference between leaving one's life according to God's timetable and taking one's own life. Suicide is not just the laying down of the body. It is the tragic loss of the divine plan of the soul, the discarded opportunity to participate in God's grand design.

To commit suicide, then, is to deny *life*: one's own life, one's own Higher Self and the life plan that would have unfolded. This plan of life is cut short—with disastrous consequences for the soul and to those who are connected with that soul as part of the divine plan.

Suicide—A National Epidemic

Suicide is on the rise. The World Health Organization estimates that approximately one million people die each year by taking their own life. In the last forty-five years, suicide rates have increased by sixty percent worldwide.

It is estimated that, on average, one person in the United States commits suicide every eighteen minutes, while as many as twenty-four others survive an attempted suicide. Suicide is now the third leading cause of death in young people age fifteen to twenty-four. In 1999 more teenagers and young adults died from suicide than from cancer, heart disease, AIDS, birth defects, stroke and chronic lung disease *combined*.

Teen suicide is approaching epidemic proportions in the United States. Teenagers are having more accidents, taking more drug overdoses and committing suicide more frequently than ever before. From 1952 to 1992, suicide rates among teens and young adults tripled. And while females are more likely to attempt suicide, males are four times more likely to succeed.[1]

"Nationally, suicide is the third leading cause of death among adolescents; in some cases, the number one and two killers, accidents and homicides, are viewed by many researchers as disguised suicides," says Loren Coleman, a suicide expert.

"Many drug overdoses, fatal automobile accidents, and related self-destructive eating and alcoholic disorders are uncounted teen suicides. Some researchers feel that because some suicides are hidden, unreported, or masked as one-car automobile accidents, for example, the total really may be more like twenty-five thousand young people a year."[2]

Suicide is also becoming a "way out" taken by an increasing numbers of adults. When life gets difficult, they think that it is time to "check out."

The true assessment of loss due to suicide cannot even be calculated—it devastates individuals, families, schools and communities. It is estimated that each suicide intimately affects at least six other people. It is also estimated that there are five million living Americans who at one time in their life tried to kill themselves. And the truth is that almost everyone at some time in their life has thought of committing suicide or been tempted to do so.

Suicide results from many complex factors. Depression and substance abuse are associated with a high percentage of suicides, and suicide is more likely to occur during periods of crisis—socioeconomic, family and individual—and of loss, whether loss of a loved one, loss of employment or loss of honor.

But understanding what happens to the soul who passes on after suicide can help people when they are faced with the choice of whether to take their own life or continue to live. Knowledge of spiritual truth can be a defense to protect them in times of trouble and despair.

What Happens When You Die?

When a soul passes through the veil of death, it is not really the end of life, but the beginning of a new life apart from the body. Each soul's experience after death may be different, depending on the circumstances of their death and the choices they have made in that lifetime.

After the soul has left the body, the angels may come in response to the prayers and requests of those in embodiment to take that soul to another plane of existence, which some people think of as "heaven." Angels wrap the soul in swaddling garments of light as that one is borne to homes of light in the heaven-world.

If the death was traumatic or untimely, the soul may be comforted by heavenly helpers. This is particularly true for children. Sometimes they sleep for a time in a lovely room, with plants and soft light and music that bathes the soul in the love of heaven. When ready to awaken, they are gently roused by angelic helpers and taken to schoolrooms where they can be instructed by angelic beings and masters of light.

Yes, there are schools and centers of learning in the heaven-world. In these schools, souls learn about the forces that came to bear on their life. They study the circumstances of life and family and the effect of that life on loved ones and the world. They are shown the tests they were intended to pass in that life. All of this is in preparation for the next step, the next assignment in the evolution of the soul.

But for the soul who has committed suicide, things are not quite so simple.

Every Suicide Goes to Heaven, Right?

Many of those who have gone through a near-death experience have seen glimpses of the life of the soul on other planes of existence. They often see a tunnel of light, meet angels and beings of light and experience a part of the heaven-world. However, those who have had a near-death experience due to an attempted suicide often have a very different story to tell—they find themselves in a place of darkness rather than a place of light.

Sadly, those who succeed in ending their life through suicide often do not reach the heaven-world or meet with heavenly helpers. Actually, the ones who get to heaven are the lucky ones. Many suicides do not arrive at heaven's door but spend time in the lower levels of the *astral plane*, a frequency of time and space that vibrates beneath the level of the physical world.

This level of existence has been known by different names in many cultures and religions. For example, when the Catholic Church speaks of purgatory and the Christian Bible speaks of hell, this is basically a name for the astral realm, especially the lower astral plane.

Many would-be suicides who have lived through a near-death experience report that they did not go to a place of light and comfort but were temporarily located in a darker place where they could quickly learn the lessons of rejecting the gift of life.

They were acutely aware of the pain they caused themselves and others and the problems that would ensue. Free from the numbing effects of the drugs or alcohol that were either the means of their death or often contributed to their death, they were now forced to deal directly with their feelings and issues—the very ones they hoped to escape. They did not find the surcease they sought, but found themselves in a place where despair and hopelessness were even greater than they had been in life.

For those who pass from life by suicide, this visit to the astral plane is only temporary, for once the lessons are learned, they are returned very soon to embodiment. The laws of life decree that they must come back into a new body. They must face once again the circumstances that caused them to take their life—the challenges they tried to walk away from. They must understand what took them out of embodiment, and then they must make correct choices and affirm life, not death. This may be difficult for the soul to face, but it is necessary. The soul has a debt to life that can only be balanced in the earthly realm, where the debt was made.

The soul returns to earthly parents, goes through the years of growing up and all that they entail. Then, one day, the soul will come face to face with circumstances similar to those faced before—the choice to live or not to live. This test will almost be like déjà vu. The soul will face once again all the tests she did not pass.*

The soul now has to catch up, making up for lost time. Worse still, the very pain she sought to avoid was not avoided at all. In fact, in many cases, it has been compounded.

If people knew this one fact alone, it could make an enormous difference. Many who consider suicide might well make a different choice if they knew where the decision would lead them.

*We use the pronouns *she* and *her* to refer to the soul because each soul, whether housed in a male or a female body, is the feminine counterpart of the masculine Spirit.

A Case History from the Heaven-World

Miguel* is a graphic example from the case histories of the heaven-world. He was born in Venezuela and later moved to America. He took up a spiritual path in his early twenties, making a break from his earlier life of cocaine and marijuana use.

But about three years later, he returned to South America and slid away from spiritual things and back into his old lifestyle, which proved deadly the second time around. After an overdose of cocaine, he collapsed in a hotel room and was dead on arrival at the hospital. The overdose may have been an accident or it may have been given to him by someone who intended to kill him. He was robbed after he died.

It was not until two months later that some of Miguel's

* The case histories in this book have been drawn from the files of Neroli Duffy, Marilyn Barrick and Elizabeth Clare Prophet. The names of the individuals and some details of their stories have been changed to protect their privacy and that of their families.

friends learned of his death and made the calls to Archangel Michael and the legions of blue-lightning angels for his soul. The angels needed the authority of those prayers to intercede for Miguel. They were able to pinpoint his whereabouts and found him on the astral plane, sitting in a bar. (Yes, there are bars on the astral plane.) He had been partying since he died.

As can happen, Miguel had not yet realized that he was dead, and he simply continued on the astral plane what he had been doing in the physical. Miguel saw a blue-lightning angel approach, and at that moment, seeing the angel, he realized that he was dead, that he no longer had a body. He became hysterical, almost out of his mind over the realization that he was dead.

As often happens in the case of sudden, unexpected deaths, Miguel was gently but firmly taken by the angels to a place where he could rest. His soul needed this interlude to disassociate from the events of his passing and to reintegrate his emotions, his mind and his spirit.

Miguel was hysterical because he could see the state of the earth, and he feared that he would not have another opportunity to be in embodiment, to be on a spiritual path, to make the right choices to balance his karma, his debt to life, and to win his reunion with God.

We have all heard the story of the dying man who sees his whole life flash before him. That, in fact, is true. What flashed in front of Miguel when he realized he was dead was his life, where he went off the Path, and what his future held. In seconds, he saw it all—past, present and future all in that moment. He was not in a good place, and it was going to take a lot of work to get to where he really wanted to be.

The subtlety of the force that worked upon Miguel was the force of suicide. In effect, Miguel committed spiritual suicide long before he died, and he was ripe for the dark forces that wanted his body and his light, first through cocaine and then through death. Perhaps he did not intend to die, but he consciously made the choice to walk a path where this was the end result.

What happened to Miguel should concern us all profoundly. God gives us a great deal of freedom to make our own choices in life. Miguel took that freedom for granted and thought that because he knew about the spiritual path that he had mastery of these things. He thought somehow he could play around with cocaine and still be okay. But he drifted away, not realizing that he was going into the very jaws of death. And when the moment of transition came, he did not even know, through the haze of drugs, that he had left his body.

Miguel was a likable guy. He was the life of the party and had a loving heart. But that was not enough. He had an opportunity with the gift of life that was given to him, but he squandered it knowingly.

After a short period of rest, Miguel will likely have to come back in another body, although, with the widespread practice of abortion, a body in which to be born may be hard to come by. He will have to start all over again as an infant, a baby, a toddler, all the way up to the teenage years.

If he is fortunate, he will have parents and teachers who will help him make right choices as he matures. But he will also come up against his old habits and momentums. He will face similar situations and circumstances, and he will have to learn the lessons he was meant to learn in the life he threw away.

If Miguel could talk to us now, he would say, "It was not worth it. Don't do it! Appreciate the life that you have, and learn your lessons well."

We Have Lived Before

There are multifaceted causes for suicide and for the self-destructive behavior of troubled teenagers today. We cannot simply attribute everything to one single aspect of the many complexities that surround our youth. Nevertheless, we do have to consider the element of karma and the part that momentums from past lives play in the choices made by the soul.

And while the concepts of karma and reincarnation are sometimes controversial in the West, we find that they can give us a deeper understanding of some of the complex spiritual questions of life, as well as insight into why people commit suicide and why it is such a backward step for the soul.

Take the following example from the *Washington Times* September 27, 1994, issue. James Cooke, an employee of the city of Los Angeles, retired to rural Minnesota with his wife, Lois, and their two adopted teenage daughters. He got along well with his neighbors and took a job milking cows.

In September 1994, sixty-three-year-old James discovered that Lois had told the police that he was molesting their daughters. James killed all three—shooting Lois in the back and the two girls, Holly and Nicole, as they slept in their beds. He then shot himself. In his suicide note he apologized for the killings but did not admit to molesting the girls.

Where does the soul of Mr. Cooke go when he gets to the other side? Hell or heaven? Will God really send him to burn in hell for all time? Will he ever get a chance to make up for his final desperate acts?

If there is no hell, or if God doesn't put him there, will he go to heaven? Assuming Holly, Nicole and Lois went to heaven, will they have to share their lives with their murderer for all eternity? The first alternative lacks mercy; the second lacks justice.

Only reincarnation offers a satisfactory solution: Mr. Cooke must return and give life to those whom he deprived of life. They must reembody to complete their life plans, and he must serve them to make up for the pain he caused. All four need further opportunity on earth. So do many others who die prematurely.

Many people whose religious traditions exclude reincarnation draw a blank on questions like: "Why does God allow babies and children to die? What about teenagers killed by drunken drivers? Why do they live at all if their lives are so brief?" "Why, God—why did you give me Johnny, only to allow him to be taken by leukemia?"

What are priests and ministers to say? Their training offers such bland answers as "It must be part of God's plan," or "We cannot understand his purposes." They may suggest that a beloved child who has died was here to teach us about love and has now gone to be with Jesus in heaven.

Reincarnation is a much more satisfying solution to these age-old questions about life. The principles of karma and reincarnation can help us understand many of life's challenges. With a deeper understanding of our own place in the universe, we develop a new understanding of the impact of suicide.

Life is not a spectator sport. We reap what we have sown—yesterday, five minutes ago and ten thousand years ago. But we do not always reap what we have sown immediately. God has ordained the cycles and laws of his universe, and many of us do not reap in a given lifetime what we have sown in that life. But at the right time, as cycles turn, the energy we have sent out will come full circle.

Suicide is a major karma-making choice. We make karma with everyone we hurt by that self-destructive action—

including our own soul. And karmic law dictates that we return to life immediately to rectify that error in judgment and to serve those whom we have hurt by our actions.

In the New Testament we read, "God is not mocked. Whatsoever a man soweth that shall he also reap."[3] This means that we can't ignore God's law of karma or think that it does not apply to us. Whatever we send out will eventually come due.

If at the conclusion of a lifetime we wind up with a large karmic debt to be paid, as is the case with suicide, God sends us back to make things right. Reembodiment is a merciful solution when compared with the idea that it's either heaven or hell at the end of one life. Reincarnation gives us the opportunity to come back again, to make amends and to complete our mission.

Some of the most compelling evidence for reincarnation comes from the past-life memories of children and teenagers. These experiences are far more common than we think, and many children, even at an early age, spontaneously recall details of their past lives—their families and occupations, what happened to them the last time they died, their life's experiences. Often it is just a small slice of a past-life experience that is recalled.

Seven-year-old Celia came running to her mother one afternoon and exclaimed excitedly, "Mommy, I remember something I did before!" "What do you mean, sweetheart?" her mother asked.

Celia explained, "I was playing with Sofi [her puppy], and all of a sudden I was sitting on a hill watching a city burn down. And I was big, like you. How can I be in two places at the same time?"

Her mother was puzzled. She asked Celia, "Was anyone with you on the hill?" "No, I was all by myself, but I wasn't scared. I was just watching the fire. It's like I couldn't do anything about it. And the important thing is, I had another body, a grown-up body!"

Celia's mother knew about past-life experiences, so she asked her daughter to tell her what being in another body felt like. Celia thought for a moment, "Well, it was okay—I didn't think about it until I got back here. Mom, do you think it was another life I had?"

"What do you think?" asked her mother. Celia quickly responded, "Well, that's exactly what I think! Thanks, mom." And Celia was off playing with her puppy again.*

Adults, too, may spontaneously catch a glimpse of a past

*A book by Carol Bowman, *Children's Past Lives: How Past Life Memories Affect Your Child*, offers many real-life examples and fascinating evidence of past-life memories in children.

life. In a spiritual study group, while meditating, John experienced being part of a solemn procession of Franciscan monks. At the same time, a woman in the group experienced observing him in the procession from her cloistered position as a nun. When the meditation came to an end, John shared this moving experience and the woman joined in, offering her perspective of the very same event. They agree that it is too coincidental to be anything but a past-life experience.

Many people have also recalled past-life memories through the use of hypnosis, and studies using hypnosis have provided much insight into how past-life momentums and memories can affect people.

However, while important findings have resulted from these studies, there are dangers in actively seeking to find out about our past lives, especially through using hypnosis as a means to that end. Hypnosis, even when used with the best of intentions, can make us spiritually vulnerable—it can open us to elements of the subconscious and unconscious of the practitioner. In addition, through hypnosis we may prematurely uncover records of events from past lives when we are not ready to deal with them. It is far better to allow our Higher Self to reveal to us what we need to know, if and when we need to know it.

Tests Faced Before

An interesting finding from the study of the past life memories of children and adults is that sometimes a person who attempts or commits suicide in this life has faced this same test in a previous life. If this is the case, it can definitely influence how the individual will react this time around.

Each time we commit a negative act, we initiate a momentum. And each time we repeat a particular negative act, it is like winding another coil on an electromagnet. For an electromagnet, the number of turns of the wire determines the strength of the magnet. In a similar way, the number of times we repeat a negative act determines the strength of the negative habit. It is like reinforcing a coil of negative energy around the core of being. The habit becomes harder and harder to break.

In studying past lives, we find that there are people who have committed suicide lifetime after lifetime. And this possibility is something we need to consider when we are dealing with people who are feeling the pressure of suicide.

Jake, a young man in his early twenties, remembers taking his life the last time around and believes he has done it in other lifetimes as well. In this life he is determined not to give in to suicidal thoughts, but he is troubled with depression and self-deprecation. Although he has set his feet firmly on the upward path and doesn't want to repeat his error, he is discovering that it is difficult to beat the depression.

The only time Jake experiences relief is when he focuses on his prayers and spiritual work. When he invokes enough of God's light, he feels an almost instantaneous uplift, which lasts for some time. But if he forgets his spiritual practice, then the depression comes creeping in again.

This is a karmic condition, of which Jake is fully aware, and he is determined to overcome this challenge and to follow a different course in this life. That determination, combined with his spiritual work, will likely bring him the victory if he remains vigilant. But his battle against depression will last many years and perhaps all his life, depending on how strong the momentum.

We can see illustrated in Jake's experience the universal law of karma, which requires that sooner or later people who commit suicide will come to the place where they must face the same test again. Momentums of the past can and must be overcome. The cycle must be broken. If it is not, then another turn is wound on the coil, and it will take more effort to overcome the pull of suicide in the next life.

However, we can't use momentums from past lives as an out. We cannot simply say, "Well, I have done this before and that is why I am doing it now. This is just the way I am." We can have compassion and understand why someone may be tempted, but we can't use this as an excuse. Self-destructive cycles and patterns *can* be broken and new roads formed and taken.

However, it takes work at all levels of being—mental, emotional and physical, as well as spiritual.

The Soul Desires to Pass Her Tests

It is said that God does not give us any more than we can handle in life or any tests that we cannot pass.

Prior to this life, we were instructed by angels and masters of light. The angels informed us of the tests we must pass and they also informed us of the exact equation of the karma we must balance. If we have failed the test of suicide in a past life, they have said to us: "This time you must stand, face and conquer the energy and momentum of suicide. You must affirm life and make the decision not to end your life.

"There will be people to help you, but you must do your part. You must resist the temptation to take what seems to be the easy way out. Then you must go on and fulfill your divine plan in joy and great love. There are many souls waiting for you who will need your love and help."

It is a pity that we do not receive an instruction manual for life when we are born, for the preparation was thorough and detailed. And yet our Higher Self and soul contain the knowledge at inner levels, and it can be accessed through prayer and internal direction. If we are attentive, we will see that the circumstances of life also contrive to teach us these lessons.

Judy, a young woman who was celebrating her coming of age at twenty-one, got in with a wild crowd and overdosed on a combination of alcohol and barbiturates. She had enough good karma that while she was unconscious, her soul was taken to the octaves of light and she was reminded of her promises to God before this lifetime. Her mission had been to rescue other souls caught in similar circumstances. Instead, she had become so despondent about her own predicament that she had given up.

She was very upset when she realized what she had done. She begged God for an immediate opportunity to mend her ways. Her spiritual advisors warned Judy that even though she understood the instruction, she must face the test again.

By the time her therapist, Marilyn, reached the hospital, Judy had regained consciousness and was feeling terrible physically, but determined emotionally. The doctors had been able to save her life, but she knew it was up to her to save her soul. So as soon as she was able to think somewhat clearly, she and Marilyn worked out a strategy.

Marilyn gave Judy a pretty strong dose of tough love, which she accepted. She promised to heed the instruction of her spiritual advisors and she committed to begin attending meetings of Alcoholics Anonymous (AA) and Narcotics Anonymous (NA). She said, "I know it's going to be tough, but I have some great spiritual advisors upstairs. I can't afford to let them or myself down again."

Judy would start each day by affirming her desire to live and giving her prayers and calls for the clearing of the momentum of suicide and the forces of darkness behind it. And when the going got rough, she was as good as her word. Every time she began to weaken or feel sorry for herself, she would contact her AA or NA sponsor for support or call Marilyn for another dose of stern but loving "Dutch uncle" talk.

Once she was on the road to recovery, Judy began to offer the help she had received to another girl, Pamela, who was facing similar challenges. They made a pact to be there for each other.

Judy called recently to say that she is still on planet Earth and feeling pretty good about herself. She is twenty-five years old now, and as she put it, she and Pamela are still "on the straight and narrow." They are regular attendees at NA and

AA and jointly sponsor a young girl who reminds them of where they were four years ago.

Judy has put her wild-crowd experience into perspective: "That period in my life was a coming-of-age party I regret, but it was also a strong wake-up call I've heeded. God gave me another chance, and I'm not going to let him or myself down."

Your soul is aware of the tests you must pass and desires very much for you to pass them. She knows the end from the beginning. Your soul knows why you took embodiment, why you chose the family you were born into, and why you need to be with the people you meet and work with every day. Your soul knows who you are intended to fall in love with and marry and the souls you will bring in as children in your own family.

Your soul also knows the challenges you will face and how to overcome them. She knows exactly the karma that you have agreed to balance and even how to balance it.

With your spiritual advisors, you planned everything in surprising detail before you were born. Many times, you chose the difficult circumstances you face in life precisely because you knew it would be the best way to get through those problems quickly and balance the most karma.

A Package on the Doorstep Every Day

We have talked about karma as a key element in understanding suicide, and karma is a word that has crept into the vocabulary these days. But what exactly is karma? And how does it work?

Karma is the law of cause and effect—as we sow, so shall we reap. All that we do, think and feel has results in the world in which we live.

When we throw a pebble into a pond, the ripples go out to the farthest shore. So it is in our lives. All of life is energy, and energy is neither created nor destroyed. We all affect the world, even as the world affects us, and what we send out to others returns to us, often gathering more of its kind before it comes home to roost.

If we send out love and kindness, then love and kindness will return to us on the gentle currents of the universal ebb and flow. If we engage in harmful or unkind behavior, that negative energy also returns to us for balancing, often as waves crashing against the shore of our being.

At the end of each day, the recording angels tally up our score. Are we in the black or in the red in the ledger of life? Each day we have the opportunity to make positive or negative karma through good or bad thoughts, feelings, actions and words. The choice is ours alone, and God does not interfere with our free will. He wants us to experience the consequences of our decisions.

We make negative karma when we send out harmful thoughts and feelings, when we do harmful and unkind acts, when we use unkind and hurtful words. We can also make karma by acts of omission—when we don't speak up or act when we should, when we allow opportunities to pass us by.

We make good karma by helping and serving others; by giving love and compassion and sending out peaceful thoughts; by taking right steps and taking a stand for truth; and by defending life, especially when life is helpless.

Although the universe requires that all the negative energy we have sent out must return to us, the mercy of God allows this karma to not return all at once. (If it did return all at once, most of us would be in a sorry state—or not in embodiment at all.) But each day the angels deliver to our doorstep a small package of our karmic debt. If we balance this package of karma each day, we can make great progress. If we allow these increments of karma to pile up, they can eventually overwhelm us.

The whole universe runs in cycles—from the orbits of stars and planets to the processes in atoms and cells. And just as we see cycles in operation in life all around us, so there are cycles in cosmos for the return of karma. These cycles unfold in an orderly fashion like clockwork throughout our life.

Children usually do not have to deal with their karma until they reach the age of twelve. They have twelve years to become accustomed to life on earth, to prepare for the assignments that are to come, to become grounded in spiritual law and to develop an understanding of the meaning of love—all of this in preparation for the tests awaiting them.

Jesus discoursing with the teachers in the temple is the sign of this age—the soul who has learned the fundamentals of the Path and the spiritual principles of life. It is marked in Judaism by the bar mitzvah and in some Christian churches by the ritual of confirmation.

At the age of twelve, the first increment of karma descends, often heralding the difficulties of the teenage years that follow. It is no accident that we notice the onset of problems during the teenage years, but with the increment of karma comes additional light to meet and overcome that karma. If the child and the parents are aware of returning karma, they can meet it with prayer and spiritual work, with love and understanding.

On the fourteenth birthday, we find that there is a specific mastery to be gained over the karma coming due at this age. This is an increment of karma that is a momentum of fear and doubt, including all past records of the experience and the initiation of death.

At this age, the adolescent often faces a great deal of torment in coming to grips with these past-life records of death. It is a time when young people across the world find themselves considering suicide and the forms of violence that can come when they do not understand that their present problems may stem from age-old momentums.

Fortunately, at this age the teenager also has greater access to the Higher Self. The teen and parents hopefully will be aware of the Higher Self and guardian angels and will work with them. They will need that assistance to deal with the challenges of these years.

The Impulse to Self-Destruct

Jim was a fourteen-year-old boy who had a subconscious self-destructive bent he didn't recognize. It came to a head in a series of disasters: first, recklessness on the ski slopes, which gave him a broken leg; second, a serious whiplash from an accident during a joy ride with the family car (no license, only a learner's permit); third, an extreme and almost lethal reaction to marijuana, during which he hallucinated and almost didn't come out of it. After this episode, Jim would periodically reenter a hallucinatory state even though he was no longer taking marijuana or any other drug.

Jim's mom made an appointment for him to see Marilyn, and Jim was shook up enough to keep it. He was honest about his situation, which was a good start. He explained: "I don't know exactly what happens, but it's like I get on a high and it takes over, and pretty soon I'm out of control. It's worse since I did pot, which I think was laced with some other drug. But what scares me the most is that I can't control the highs—they come out of nowhere and I'm not doing any more drugs. Do you think God is punishing me?"

It was obvious that this young man's life was on its way to disaster. He was going to need both psychological and spiritual help. Marilyn explained that God wasn't punishing him, that he had put himself on "self-destruct"—but he could turn that around. In the course of his therapy, which he took seriously, she told him a story from her own life.

When she was fourteen, she was intrigued by Charles Sheldon's book *In His Steps*, in which the pastor of a church and a number of his parishioners decide that for one year they will not take any major action without asking themselves, "What would Jesus do?" That simple question turned that church upside down and right side up.

Marilyn decided that she, too, would ask herself before taking action, "What would Jesus do?" When she prayed and asked Jesus to help her know what to do, she always knew exactly what He would do. But she didn't always want to do it. She realized that was the part of herself that was leading her astray, so she decided to put her hand in Jesus' hand and confront it.

As she explained to Jim, "That was an important year in my life, walking and talking with Jesus. I won some; I lost some. But I grew up a lot, spiritually and emotionally. And to this day, when I'm in doubt as to right action, I ask myself, 'What would Jesus do?'"

Jim was thoughtful about that story, and he decided to get serious about making some changes in his life. He said, "Jesus is important to me, too. I don't know whether I can do what you did, but I get the point. I'd like to turn my life around before I accidentally kill myself. And I'm sure Jesus agrees with that."

From that time on, Jim worked hard and brought to therapy whatever situation he needed help with. He came to realize that it was the thrill factor that was driving him, and he decided to stop getting his thrills in a self-destructive way. It took a lot of prayer, self-examination and practice before he was able to catch himself in the act of self-destructing—and then to see it coming and not let it happen at all.

He also needed to change the crowd he was running with, and his parents helped him (to his chagrin) by forbidding him any contact with them. Jim focused on athletics in high school as a way to channel his high energy. He also did his spiritual work (through prayer and some of the spiritual techniques we will discuss in this book). And he kept his grades up because his parents made that stipulation if he wanted to keep doing sports.

When he concluded his therapy a year later, he was graduating from high school with a B+ average—and headed for college. His out-of-control highs were a thing of the past. He said, "I'm really glad my folks put their foot down, and that you were honest with me, too. I'm feeling pretty good about turning that self-destruct attitude around—I've got a lot to live for!" When Marilyn congratulated him, he said, "I've always appreciated what you told me about you and Jesus. He's been a good friend to me, too."

There is a descent of spiritual energy at age fourteen, an increment of God-mastery that is intended to be a walk with Jesus. The master Jesus walked the earth and lived through his adolescent years, even as young people do today. His childhood at his mother's knee and learning carpentry at the side of his father, Saint Joseph, was an important period of training that shaped the boy who became the man and then the master.

The understanding of the life of Christ can be a tremendous bulwark in the life of the adolescent, the teenager or the adult—the understanding of the teachings of Jesus, his words and his counsel. There is a very intimate communion we can have with Jesus that gives us the strength to meet our challenges, to walk in the way of mastery, and even to overcome the temptation to commit suicide.

Remember that Jesus has said to us: "Be of good cheer! I have overcome the world."[4] And following in his footsteps, we can, too.

Wise parents, teachers and sponsors of youth can help children and teenagers understand and develop a very personal relationship with this beloved master.

Reckless Abandon

Deliberately setting out to kill oneself (and often others in the process) is totally alien to healthy young people, but the forces of suicide have ploys that can entrap the most sophisticated soul. And underneath, we sometimes find that the reckless abandon that can overtake young people flags a subconscious mindset that is essentially suicidal.

However, this is not the way the young person sees it. Someone caught in this state of consciousness usually explains a dangerous activity as "something exciting, an adventure, a rush." At a physical level, the adrenaline surge can become addictive—and the thrill, psychologically addictive. At that point, like any other addiction, the person has lost a measure of free-will control—his choices are now driven by the addiction itself.

It is certainly true that people sometimes face choices in life where they are called to do dangerous things, but this is a very different thing from the daredevil consciousness. For example, a marine on the front lines or on a dangerous mission might have a probability of death that some might consider an agreement to suicide. Yet this is not suicide, but the ultimate sacrifice: the laying down of one's life for one's friends. In these cases a life plan is not aborted. Indeed, it may be in accordance with the life plan of a soldier that he manifest a greater love in laying down his life for his country and also that his fellow soldiers might live. These selfless acts are not thought of as suicide and do not have the karma of suicide.

The daredevil consciousness is very different from this—it is risking one's life just for the very thrill of it, for the sense of "cheating death." The influence of the force of suicide that accompanies these thrill-seeking activities is strong and potentially life threatening unless the young person sees the drama for what it is. And the popularization of these activities by the entertainment industry doesn't help. Sadly, in the twenty-first century, there is a relative dearth of entertainment that promotes higher values—including the value of life itself.

We are seeing a breakdown in moral and social values in many cultures worldwide. This downward spiral influences all of us, especially the youth whose lives must play out in the midst of a cultural malaise. All of this is grist for the mill for suicide.

Depression, Discouragement and Despair

Suicide often follows on the heels of depression—a sense of hopelessness or despair, an inability to see anything positive about life. Everyone gets sad sometimes. We all have disappointments, and grief over a loss is a normal and healthy reaction. But when sadness turns to hopelessness or despair, when a person can no longer see anything positive about life, and when these feelings last for a long time, then there is cause for concern.

Depression is a medical and psychological condition that can result from a number of causes—including illness, biochemical or bodily imbalances, or an unhealthy reaction to challenges in life. Left untreated, it can lead to poor health, despair and ultimately to suicide.

Depression can be seen by clairvoyants as a syrupy, dark substance in the aura and a downward flow of energy in the body. It can also be seen as a literal depression of the spiritual centers in the body. These centers should be filled with light, but in the depressed or suicidal person, they are concave, or literally "caved in" or "depressed."

While depression can have an internal source, it can also be the result of external circumstances or negative energies impinging upon us. It may very well occur in the teens when life takes a downward turn: someone hurts our feelings or one of our friends lets us down or our parents have a fight or school work seems over our head or we fail ourselves in some way.

Any one of these circumstances is tough to handle. And if we can't figure out how to make it better, we can become depressed. And this is true not only for teens and adults; children can also fall prey to depression and suicide.

Brian, a nine-year-old boy despondent over problems his parents were having, took sleeping pills from the medicine cabinet and deliberately overdosed. He got scared when he started feeling woozy, so he told his teenage brother what he had done. The teenager immediately woke up his parents, who rushed the boy to the hospital.

The family doctor met them and saw to it that Brian's stomach was pumped. With the parents' permission, the pump was left in a bit longer than necessary so that Brian would understand that a suicide attempt has physical consequences. Hopefully, he would not want to try it again. The parents also took their son's suicide attempt seriously. They worked on resolving their problems and followed up with their own therapy.

Depression is something that we all face from time to time and in different degrees. Often it comes at times of difficult life circumstances, especially in situations of change or loss—of a friend, a loved one, a job or any significant element of life. It can also come during "down-time," when we don't have the usual routines and rhythm of life.

A teacher in his thirties, who was much loved by his students and seemed to have everything going for him, committed suicide over the Christmas holidays. Of all the times in the year that this might happen, one wouldn't expect it to be at Christmas. And yet, unfortunately, this is not unusual.

As psychologists and ministers explain it, hopes and ideals are highlighted at this time of year, and the contrast between the ideal and the actuality of a person's circumstances can be discouraging. This is especially true for those who must spend Christmas alone. Sadly, the ultimate outcome can be despair—and a suicide attempt.

We all deal with sadness, loss and grief. And many people

have the "blues" from time to time. But for a few people, this becomes a spiral that goes only downward and ends in depression. Whatever its cause, depression is debilitating to our body and soul. Thus, it is important that depression that lasts more than two weeks or that seriously affects a person's life be treated with professional help (and with medication if necessary).

Sweet Death

We are all aware of the obvious cases of suicide, where people take action to end their life in a sudden way. But there are also more subtle forms of suicide.

Some people find themselves entranced into deeper and deeper levels of a self-hypnotized death. Their death is insidious because it is gradual. It is a slipping away from selfhood while the body and the surface senses are still in motion. It is a death of awareness, of sensitivity to life—of the will to be.

This gradual process of self-destruction is called "sweet death." Many young people live with the daily spectacle of this sugarcoated death. Self-deluded, they fail to realize that there is no longer a free choice, the freedom to choose to be or not to be—life or death. Life is no longer Real. The only choice is what color, what flavor, death?

Then there is "slow-motion suicide." If we are honest, we

will realize that wrong choices in our life can lead to suicide. There are many ways to shorten our lives. These can involve wrong diet, over- or under-eating, drinking alcohol, using nonprescription drugs, smoking—there are many habits that shorten our lifespan.

In the light of spiritual understanding, we need to look at the choices we make to see if they affirm life. If they do not, then we would be wise to forsake them and replace them with habits and choices that will give us the strength and vitality to live a long life of love, compassion and service to others.

Self-Destructive Lifestyles

Death comes in many disguises. People are killing themselves every day willfully and knowingly through addictions, squandering the life force, not paying attention to health, eating food they know is not good for them, being negative in thoughts and feelings, spewing out hatred and receiving it on the return current. They take a chance with death by taking unnecessary risks, driving dangerously, and generally "living on the edge." There are so many ways in which people can deny life.

Basically, these negative habits are a form of conscious or unconscious self-destruction, and they herald hidden self-hatred or despondency. The downward spiral is accelerated by the adrenaline rush that accompanies many of these life-shortening activities. When that adrenaline is pumping, it's difficult to realize that the seeming "high" is a path to destruction. As Joe, a teenager recovering from an overdose of amphetamines, ruefully put it, "The higher you fly, the harder you crash."

Conditions such as anorexia nervosa and bulimia can also be psychological manifestations of an impulse to suicide, often out of the control of the soul burdened by them. These behavior patterns need treatment and much prayer and spiritual work. Young people struggling to overcome these compulsive patterns also need loving understanding and moral support from friends and loved ones.

Sonja, a seventeen-year-old model, bought into this misery inadvertently. She was expected to keep a slim, sexy figure, which required constant dieting. Her body would say, "I'm starving!" so she would binge to please her body. Then she would regurgitate so she could stay slim and keep her modeling contract.

Fortunately, Sonja had an understanding boyfriend who loved her too much to let her keep following this path. He was her champion when she decided to quit modeling. And he was the one who persuaded her to tell her parents what was going on.

Everyone, including girlfriends who had talked Sonja into modeling, decided she had a lot more going for her than her figure. With the support of family and friends, Sonja made it through medical treatment and a makeover of her self-image.

The last time we heard from Sonja, she was in good spirits—and her grade-point average had gone way up. She said, "Slinky bodies are vastly overrated. I'd rather have my health and sanity. Besides that, I'm aiming for a career in social work that requires a college education. And I'm going to make that happen."

Sonja is only one of many young people who have turned a self-destructive lifestyle around. In every case, it has taken determination and hard work, but those who have made it agree that the effort was well worth it. Their lives are back on track, and their friends and the support network they have developed continue to be an extra safety belt when life gets tough.

The support of friends and loved ones, plus professional help as necessary, are important ingredients for success. If you have friends who are caught up in self-destructive lifestyles, let them know that they can turn things around—and help them get the help they need to win their victory.

So Recently in Heaven

If you talk to young people, many will tell you that they long for the purity they once knew. It may be a longing for the innocence of childhood, but it is also a memory of prior experiences in the octaves of light.

It is hard for the soul who has come so recently from the heaven-world to live in the earthly plane with all its imperfections. When you have seen at inner levels the worlds God designed in the Beginning, when you have been shown the purpose and the plan for life, when a latent memory of perfection and love stirs within the mind, it is indeed painful to be on earth, to see the wars and the tragedies and know that this was not meant to be. This is one factor that contributes to increasing suicidal tendencies in children, teenagers and young adults.

There are many souls coming into embodiment who are destined to be Christs and Buddhas unto all mankind, avatars of great light. They come with a mission and a high calling, and they must be protected. For the world does not understand their light and often condemns them.

Heaven is very concerned about these souls, for when such souls have been sent forth in the past, many have been lost. Many came of age not knowing who they were or why they were here. Some committed suicide because they could not stand to be in the turmoil of a world so different from the world of light they had recently come from. The angels watched in horror as these souls were lured into drugs and self-destruction.

If these young souls should give way to disillusionment, besides being vulnerable to despair, they could also be led astray. It is altogether understandable that young people are sometimes caught up in the spirit of revolution that is led by Antichrist. They seek to overthrow all that they see because it does not agree with the inner concept they know to be true.

Hopelessness and anger are two possible reactions to the darkness of the world, but a better way is to face the world with compassion, tolerance and a determination to make a difference. It is important to pray that these souls of great light—and the souls of all children—be given the guidance they need from parents, teachers and mentors so that they can find a higher way. Pray that they survive the difficult childhood and teenage years so that they can offer their gifts to the world and fulfill their divine plan.

Pray especially for the babies in the womb and the little ones in their childhood years. Up to the age of seven, there is the great opportunity of sealing them in the fires of the Christ and the light of the Buddha. Whatever is impressed upon the clay of consciousness during the period of formation in the womb and the first seven years is most important.

We can call for the protection of the angelic hosts. If we daily invoke protection for the children of the world, that is all the angels need to step into the earthly plane and intercede. They have promised to answer our calls. We have the authority for this world, and until we ask, the angels cannot come forth to do the bidding of the Father.

Pray that these little ones be sealed in the immaculate concept, in the divine design of the heart of God. Pray that their divine plan be fulfilled in their lives. See them enveloped in the white light of purity. Call for the sealing action of the Sacred Heart of Jesus and the World Mother around these blessed ones. By doing so, we can all render a great service.

An Interview with Angie Fenimore

Angie Fenimore had a near-death experience when she attempted to commit suicide. She came back from that experience, and her life was turned around. She wrote a book called Beyond the Darkness: My Near-Death Journey to the Edge of Hell and Back, *which describes her experiences.*

In the following excerpt from a radio program, Elizabeth Clare Prophet interviews Angie. As she speaks of her experiences, we can learn a great deal about the spiritual equation of suicide.

Q: We've all heard the stories of those who have passed beyond the veil and come back to tell us what heaven is like. But today our guest is Angie Fenimore, whose near-death experience took her to the edge of hell and back again.

Angie, you are a wife and mother who had a harrowing near-death experience when you attempted to commit suicide. Miraculously you were restored to life, and I am certain that many, many people have benefited from that miracle in your life, so please tell us about it.

A: Oh, sure. I'd had just a really tragic childhood, a lot of really horrible things that happened to me that I kind of just stuffed inside—I didn't really deal with them at all. And it wasn't until I was married and had a couple of children that memories started resurfacing, and I struggled with that. I went to a support group for survivors of sexual abuse, which was just one of the many things that happened to me.

For me, just hearing the stories of other survivors made my pain actually deeper. I felt like my problems were different from the other women that I spoke with, and I really started to turn inward and just cut myself off from other people and kind of lived a separate reality. I'd still go grocery shopping and see my friends but they had no idea what was going on inside of me. I don't think anybody really did, even my husband.

And I just came to a point where I felt like I couldn't overcome this, I just couldn't, and I was terrified that I was going to pass these horrible traits on to my children, that they were going to suffer from the same kind of depression that I suffered from and that they were just all better off without me.

It was January, I had gone to the grocery store, a little convenience store. We lived in Okinawa, Japan, at the time and this was just a little shop on base, and I didn't even bother to change out of my sweats and slippers. I went in my slippers and grabbed the milk, and I went home and I pulled into the parking space, but I could not make myself go in the house. I just couldn't do it.

So I just left. I pulled out and found a place to hole up for the night. The next day I went to a movie, went shopping and got myself some shoes and some clothing and washed my hair in the sink in the bathroom and I didn't call home. I didn't let anybody know where I was. I just felt this terrible, deep need to escape, and it would not go away no matter what I did.

When I finally went home, I was floored, I was devastated by what I'd put my family through. I couldn't believe that I was capable of hurting them that deeply. And I think it was later that night, when everybody else went to sleep and I stayed up all night, that I decided that I just wasn't going to put them through it any more.

So I slit my wrists and took a bottle of pills, which came back up. And so I went and dug through my medicine cabinet and took everything that was in there just kind of slowly—just kept taking it so it wouldn't come back up, and sent my kids off to a neighbor when it was a decent hour. And that was when it happened.

Q: That must have been a most profound turning point in your life, reaching the depths of hell and then climbing back up again and living to tell the tale.

A: Well, what happened to me was I had had a stepmother who'd had a near-death experience and shared it with me, but it was before anybody had even talked about near-death experiences, so I wasn't sure whether even to believe her or if what she had experienced was true. It happened when I was just very young before she knew me, and I was probably fourteen when she told me about it.

And what she had told me was that she had been in a car accident, and when she died she went up to the corner of the room and she was greeted by beings of light who told her she wasn't done, that she still had a mission here, but she was given a choice.

And so that's what I expected when I laid down on the couch. I felt just this intense power, very, very powerful energy, stronger than I can even describe really, and I couldn't tell whether it was in the room or just within me.

Q: What's the first thing that happened to you after you went out of your body? How did it make you feel?

A: Well, because of what my stepmother told me, I was expecting to see myself down on the couch from up in the corner of the room. And so I opened my eyes as I felt this energy pull me out of my body. I knew I'd left my body. But when I opened my eyes, I was pulled back in, and this happened to me a few times. Then I realized that I had to exercise my own will to make this happen, that it wasn't a natural thing and that I was going to have to force it. So I just really concentrated very hard—and that's when it happened.

The first thing that happened to me was I went directly into my life review, starting with my birth. But it was from everybody's perspective—my mother's, everybody's. And that was probably the most interesting thing for me, because I remembered things entirely differently as an adult than they had actually unfolded for me in my life, and I was shown that my parents loved me, that they struggled like everybody struggles and made mistakes like everybody does.

Then, when my life review was over, I felt a presence with me, there was somebody there with me that I couldn't see, but I swung my head around to look. I was surrounded by this darkness, and it was a thick, foreboding entity. It wasn't just an absence of light. This had an energy, a very powerful energy about it. And as I looked around for the people to be there, what I saw was a line of teenagers standing next to me. And as I leaned over and looked at them, I thought to myself, "Oh, my gosh, we're the suicides," because I could see in their faces that they were just dead in every sense of the word, that there was no hope, there was no life or energy. And from the way they were dressed I could tell that they listened to the same kind of music that I listened to, this very dark kind of music, alternative kind of stuff.

And I realized that my thoughts were audible. I wasn't sure at first that that's what was happening. But as I thought this, it was out there, and the guy standing next to me turned to look at me—and that was it and then he looked away. And there was just nothing, nothing there.

Q: In your book you say that music plays a very important role in your attempted suicide and the suicides of others. How important is music really?

A: Everything has a spiritual creation before it has a physical creation, including music. And we all have within us a measure of darkness or of light, and this is constantly changing. Music is a very powerful tool in altering that balance within us and within the space that we inhabit—we usually just can't see this darkness and light. But when I came back I could see it. I can see it in people now. But if I'm not in tune and doing everything I know I need to be doing, then that leaves me as well.

When music that is inspired by God is played, the energy changes and light comes into that area, into that space. And probably the very spirits who inspired it, or even just spirits of light, will be there.

And that is what happens when music of darkness is

played as well. It is inspired by darkness. It is inspired by Satan. He is a very real being, and he has just countless angels at his beck and call. He's very organized. And so what happens is when we play this music, these spirits gather; it is an invitation.

Q: You had a turning point where you saw a single pinpoint of light. Tell us about that.

A: After I saw the teenagers, I was taken to a different place and there were just so many people there that were filled with darkness. I looked around at them and then realized that I heard a voice, and these other people didn't hear this voice. And as I turned to look where this voice was coming from, it was just an incredible power that accompanied it, and I could feel the energy around me saying, This is God, this is God.

They were worshiping him, these little particles of energy, and as he spoke I could see where he was coming from. It looked like a single star out there, and he said, "Is this what you really want?" And he came toward me with incredible speed, but he stopped some distance from where I was.

Where I was, it was very dark and I could tell that he couldn't come in to this place. I didn't know whether it was that he wouldn't or that he couldn't, but he was maybe fifty feet from me. I was just in awe. I couldn't believe it, but I knew that this was God. I knew it was him.

It was incredible, this feeling of love that I had from him. It was like I was his daughter. And I had never felt or understood that in my life, even with all of the religious experiences I had had. I had gone to many churches, but I had felt that I was different from everybody else. They felt at home and at peace there—and I was just the adopted daughter that kind of went.

What I felt from him was an all-encompassing, all-knowing kind of love. It wasn't that he loved me for what I had done that was right or good; it was that he loved me in spite of everything. And he knew everything. There was an omniscient kind of feeling about him.

And I said to him, "My life is so hard, I can't do it, I can't go on. What else could I have done?" And he said, "This is the worst thing that you could have done"—taking my own life.

And then I was shown incredible things, and it was more like I just knew—I was just opened up to this light, this energy. And it's all the same thing—light, love, all that is good, knowledge—everything is all a wavelength of light, and this is how this information travels, on wavelengths of light.

I was shown what I was doing here: I was really on an errand, I was on a mission. I had a job to do, and my children's lives would be altered dramatically without me here, especially if I took my own life. It would be different if I were taken, but the pain and the anguish that suicide causes those people who are left is so tremendous.

I gathered from the others around me, that some of them were mumbling and just caught in a moment. And looking back now, I'm sure that many of them were just going on and on about how their life has been worthless and pointless and that suicide was their only choice, just like I was saying.

Q: Is there any hope for those who are trapped on that plane of existence?

A: Well, it's not a permanent state. This was like a place where you come to understand the gravity of the things that you've done while you're here.

Everything has impact. Everything helps to determine not only your own destiny but the destiny of others, and in order to move on you have to appreciate that, you have to feel that weight or that gravity.

Q: You know, Angie, many people think that their lives don't count, that they're really not important people and one of the things that I think that you were trying to say in your book was that everybody's life does count and that you influence many, many other people.

A: Right. One of Satan's greatest tools is to tell us that we're not important and that nothing matters. But I was shown that it is absolutely the opposite, that every little decision we make has tremendous impact and that we affect everybody in our circle, and those people in turn affect people in their circles, and those people in turn affect other people. And in that way we pass this light or this dark energy, whichever it is we choose to pass on, which is why it's so important to correct those things that we do that are mean or thoughtless.

Q: In other words, what doesn't seem like such a big deal may have much larger ramifications than most people imagine.

A: Right, and you know, it depends on the individual as well whom you're affecting, how they're going to receive it. I mean, we have responsibility on both ends—what kind of energy we are going to send out and how we are going to receive. I think there's a scripture that says that the person who is offended is a fool as well. So we have a responsibility as well to recognize that we can take in all of these things from other people but we have a choice. We can alter that and change it and send out positive energy. We don't have to take in darkness and send out darkness. It's very hard.

Q: What do you think about Satanic music and Satanism, especially in the United States these days?

A: Oh, I am so surprised that people don't see where it all begins, and it's even the top forty stuff that we listen to that is very dark as well.

I can see that there's this pattern that began many years ago in the fifties when music with a beat was first introduced. It's like we're led along. The parents of those teenagers that listened to Elvis Presley were appalled and shocked by what their kids were listening to. And then those kids grew up and were accepting of that music. And then the music of the seventies, which was just a little bit darker, was introduced. And they were appalled and shocked by what their children were listening to and then those children grew up.

And now what we have eventually is this music that is so dark that it absolutely flushes out all light. There is no room for light. And I don't think that these kids realize—and maybe some of them do realize—the power that is behind it, the energy, and that the more we succumb to that, the more power it has over us until we have no more freedom to choose for ourselves, that it will take over if we let it, if we give in to it.

Q: Angie, one of the most fascinating parts of your book, at least for me when I read it, was the fact that you have this conversation back and forth with God. And a lot of people don't mind and certainly understand if you talk to God and they think of that as prayer, but they think it's a little bit crazy if God talks to you. But this was a very natural conversation, it seemed to me. I wondered, do you still talk to God, do you have this conversation back and forth and how natural is it?

A: Well, my prayers are far more honest now. I feel like there's nothing that He doesn't know, and so there's nothing I can't share with him. I have an entirely different relationship with him now. I used to do the thing where I would say my prayers and, you know, pray for all the things that I was supposed to pray for and pretty much ignore what was really deep underneath. Now I am more honest.

PART 2

THE SPIRITUAL EQUATION

Levels of Energy

We often tend to think of suicide as a sudden action to end life. But we also see all around us people making choices and living lifestyles that are more subtle manifestations of an impulse to self-destruction.

Whether suicide is played out in a self-destructive lifestyle or in a single violent act, the untimely death is the end result of a process that began long before. There has been a shifting of energy within the person's world: from positive to negative, from optimistic to pessimistic, from life-affirming to life-denying—from light to darkness.

There are different types of energy that may be part of this process, including physical, mental and emotional energy, and all of these are related and interconnected. And there are forces that can affect the flow of this energy, both internal and external.

With an understanding of these energies and the forces

that are behind suicide, we can gain some insight into dealing with a suicide crisis. And just as importantly, we can learn to work with these energies and perhaps turn a negative spiral into a positive one *before* a crisis develops.

Your Spiritual Self

For a deeper understanding of suicide and the soul, it is important to know the elements of your spiritual being. The physical body of man and woman is what we can all see, but it is only one of the seven levels of energy or consciousness that make up the totality of who we are.

Besides your physical body, you have three other bodies that provide vehicles for your soul in the journey through time and space. These interpenetrating sheaths of consciousness are called the four lower bodies. These bodies are the physical body; the etheric or memory body, where is recorded all of your past; the mental body through which you think and cogitate; and the emotional or astral body, through which you feel.

The etheric sheath, the highest in vibration, is the gateway to your three "higher" bodies, which make up the permanent part of you that exists in the realms of Spirit. Your Christ Self (sometimes known as the Higher Self) is shown as the middle

The Chart of Your Divine Self

figure in the Chart of Your Divine Self. It is the individualized presence of the Universal principal of the Christ. It is the individual Christ consciousness that exists as potential within everyone.

Your I AM Presence surrounded by the concentric spheres of your causal body is shown as the upper figure of the Chart. This individualization of the I AM is your point of origin in the heart of God. It is the point of light and pure perfection from which your soul came out to experience life for certain cycles in the physical universe. And it is to this point that you will return when you have completed your mission here on earth.

Within your four lower bodies are seven energy centers, points of light in the body that receive and give out energy. They are called chakras. *(Chakra* is a Sanskrit term for "wheel" or "disc.") Your chakras are the internal step-down transformers that regulate the flow of God's energy to different parts of your body. The seven major chakras are positioned along the spinal column from the base of the spine to the crown.

Chakras are not static points of light but dynamic energy centers that constantly take in, send out and store spiritual light. The correct care and use of these energy centers leads to greater vitality in your physical body as well as the three finer bodies. The chakras govern the flow of energy in your four

Crown Chakra

Third-Eye Chakra

Throat Chakra

Heart Chakra

Solar-Plexus Chakra

Seat-of-the-Soul Chakra

Base-of-the-Spine Chakra

lower bodies and they affect the size and quality of your aura.

Every day we make choices as to how to use the energy God sends us through the Higher Self. It is all part of the equation of light. The daily choices we make—how we love, the words we speak, the thoughts we think and the actions we take—can influence the flow of energy in our life.

If we choose, for example, to take drugs or other harmful substances, these can cause damage not only to the physical body but also to the finer bodies. They can create holes or tears in our auric forcefield and cause us to lose the light in our spiritual centers. We can feel very alive while this is happening, because there is a flow of light and energy. But the light is lost and not easily replaced, and afterwards we can feel depleted, drained and be subject to depression. And so another dose—possibly a larger dose—is needed to

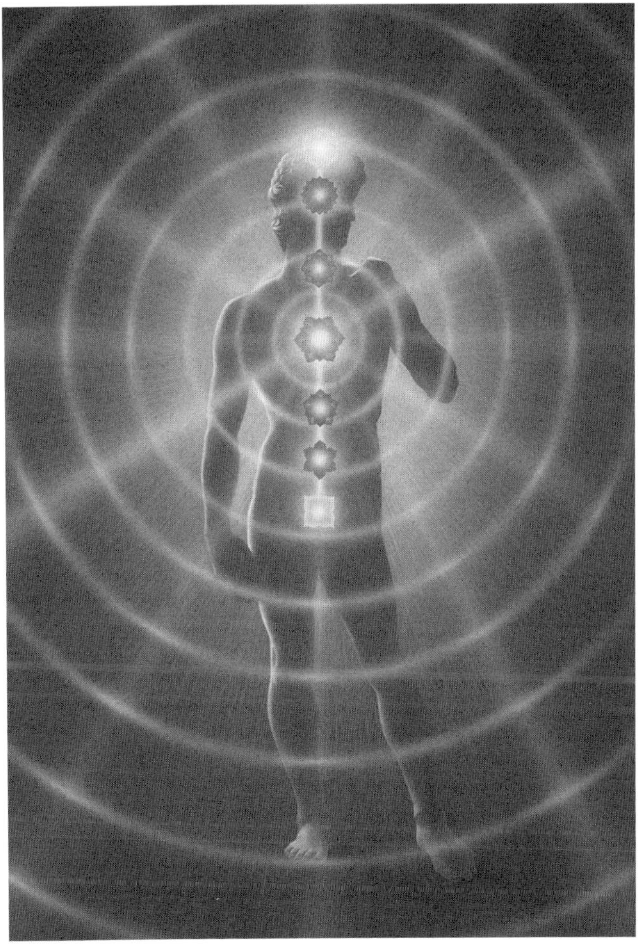

give the same high again. This can lead to a downward spiral of energy that can culminate in suicide.

The body is meant to be a holy temple, a house for the indwelling Spirit. It requires attention to diet, exercise, spiritual practice and general hygiene and appearance. What you eat affects your health, exercise gives energy and light to all of your cells, and your spiritual practice (prayer, meditation, decrees) is the driving force that propels light through the body.

The Higher Self

You have a Higher Self. It is above you right now. The angels see your Higher Self, and they know that at inner levels you are a magnificent and powerful spiritual being. Your Higher Self is sometimes called the "big me." Your Higher Self sees the big picture and never loses sight of your divine destiny. But it is your choice each day to identify with that Higher Self or not.

When you act as you know your Higher Self would act, then that Presence can draw near. You can feel that Presence, and feel God's love flowing through you. And so you can identify more and more with the Higher Self, and that Higher Self can move through you, guide and direct you. When you're confused and can't see the road ahead, remember you have a Higher Self that wants you to live and knows that better things are around the corner.

But there is also the choice not to be the Higher Self—to

identify with the selfish self, the unkind self, the angry self, the "little me." All these things are not a part of the God-Self, but are part of the *lesser self*, the limited self of human consciousness.

The knowledge that you have a Higher Self, or God-identity, and a lesser self, or human ego—and understanding when each is acting in your life—can make all the difference in your life.

So what exactly *is* this lesser self?

The Lesser Self

The lesser self is the part of ourselves that gets us into trouble. It consists of the unconscious and subconscious momentums of darkness from this life and from past lives—the lowest vibrating aspects of self. It is the antithesis of the Higher Self.

The Greater Self or the lesser self—which will it be? This is the point where an individual must choose: good or evil, light or anti-light.

It is the lesser self that gets depressed, says the unkind words and behaves badly. Although it is no part of our divine Reality, it can seem very real at times. But like an ice cube on the pavement on a hot day, the lesser self will one day disappear and be no more.

The lesser self knows that one day it will die. The Higher Self does not die, but when you finally have your victory, when you unite with the Higher Self and return to heaven, nevermore to go out, then the lesser self will be no more.

To Be—Or Not to Be

The angels see that the goal of life is for each of us to become one with our Higher Self, and yet this is a daily choice for each of us. Will we identify with our Higher Self, our Real Self, our eternal Reality? Or will we identify with the lesser self that has no permanent reality in the larger scheme of life?

There are many keys to identifying with the Higher Self. And this is what the great spiritual teachers of all ages came to show us. But perhaps the most important key is that you cannot become one with your Higher Self without giving to others. For it is in giving to others that you discover who you really are. A life that is centered on the lower self and all of its desires can only progress so far.

Our hearts are developed through loving service to others. It is especially important that young people have opportunities to serve, as this is part of the early development of the heart. Children and youth need to experience the joy of giving and come to know the meaning and purpose it holds for life. When people stop giving, then the flow of light and energy ceases. It is then that life becomes centered on the lesser self, and everything seems to lose its meaning. And that is when suicide becomes a possibility.

From a spiritual perspective, it can be clearly seen that the person who is suicidal is totally identifying with the lesser self that is destined to die and is mistakenly considering himself to be that one. Ultimately, at the root of the tendency to suicide is nonrealization of the God within. For if we truly knew that God lived within us, we would not surrender the temple of God that is our physical body until God ordained it.

But if we realize that God lives within us, then we can surrender our life to God in service to his life everywhere, and he takes care of all the details. We are able to go forward, trusting that he will care for us as we do our part. This does not mean that there will not be tough times, but with God, we can get through them.

Unseen Forces

Unseen forces that prey upon people are perhaps the most important—and the most overlooked—part of the equation of suicide.

Many people today are aware of angels and beings of light that can bring help, healing and intercession into our lives in many ways. What is not so well known is that there are also unseen forces of negativity that seek to lead people into darkness.

These forces may be personal or impersonal. They are known by different names. Many people know them as *entities*—a general name for the various types of disembodied forces of darkness. But the key to dealing with all of them is to know something of how they work and how to call to the forces of light to counteract their influence.

Disembodied Spirits

Discarnate entities are one type of entity that is often very much involved in suicide. Commonly referred to as disembodied spirits, they are made up of the personality consciousness, as it expresses through the astral, mental or etheric bodies, of those lifestreams who have passed through the change called death.

As we have seen, what happens when an individual dies depends on momentums established in life. When the physical body is laid aside, advanced souls may be taken with their other three lower vehicles (the emotional, mental and etheric bodies) to etheric temples for instruction between embodiments. But those who are not spiritually awakened find that when the crystal cord is withdrawn, the consciousness of the soul, which has identified with the lower bodies, may remain in the astral realm with the three lower bodies.

It is also possible for there to be a separation of the four lower bodies at death. In this case, the soul usually remains with the etheric body, gravitating to the etheric plane. The astral body and the mental body may wander in different realms, no longer connected to the source of life—or even to the intelligence of the soul.

These entities affinitize with those on the physical plane who have similar habit patterns to their own. Those addicted to alcohol, tobacco and drugs are examples. Wherever people congregate to indulge themselves, there the entities gather. Taverns, smoking rooms and hangouts of drug users are literally packed with discarnates who attach themselves to those who are taking in these harmful stimulants.

These entities crave the sensual pleasures to which they were addicted before losing their physical bodies. They have the same desires they had before passing through the portals of death, but they no longer have a physical body through which to experience and satisfy their desires. Thus, like leeches, they tie into the nervous systems of those who are embodied (usually at the back of the neck and along the spinal column), and by so doing they can vicariously enjoy the pleasures to which they are accustomed. This transfer takes place as the result of the merging of the astral body of the discarnate with the astral and physical bodies of a person through the sympathetic nervous system.

These evil forces are a root cause of many addictions, not only substance abuse but also addiction to sex, anger, violence or hatred. One reason that any of these things is addictive is that these negative forces attach themselves to people, attempting to influence their thoughts and feelings, continually reinforcing the craving to indulge in these habits.

There are many different kinds of discarnate entities, but they have one thing in common: they want your light. They have no connection to the Source of life and light, so they want to make you release the light of your chakras by tempting you to engage in behavior that misqualifies your energy. They fuel addictions, because this is the means by which they can access the light.

All negative habits and addictions have accompanying entities that attempt to invade the body and steal the life force. These entities include those of liquor, marijuana and other hallucinogenic drugs, tobacco, sex, sensuality, selfishness and self-adulation, anger, gossip, fear, insanity, depression, lust for money, and gambling.

There are also entities of suicide. They are attracted to those who may be depressed or despondent, magnifying and intensifying thoughts and feelings of hopelessness. They seek to entice unsuspecting souls into committing suicide as a seemingly final solution to their problems.

Negative Forces That Prey on Susceptible Individuals

The astral body disconnected from the soul and the Spirit was known to the ancient Egyptians as the *ka*. No longer under the conscious control of the soul and the Higher Self, it may wander about as a discarnate, disconnected from the soul and yet affecting others with a heavy sense of oppression or emotion. The astral ka can thus be very harmful. This is especially true in the case of a suicide, because the astral sheath of that one, being close to earth and earthbound, may return to try and influence other members of the family and relatives to commit suicide.

Harry, father of two young children, suffered from serious depression and finally succumbed to suicide. In the years following his death, his brother made several suicide attempts. Fortunately, he didn't succeed and died of natural causes a number of years later.

When Harry's wife suddenly died, the two children, now young adults, also became suicidal. One underwent successful psychiatric treatment, and the other received a strong message from Jesus. As the young man was seriously contemplating killing himself, Jesus rebuked him, "If you want to do away with yourself, give yourself to me!" He took this spiritual challenge to heart and is a devotee of Jesus today.

Friends and relatives believe that no one in this family, with the exception of Harry, really wanted to kill themselves. A likely explanation is the influence of the astral kas of those who had died, starting with Harry.

A young woman whose father, a good man who died unexpectedly after surgery, had a nightmare in which her father came rolling swiftly toward her in a wheel chair as if to run her down. The expression on his face was malevolent, stony and unreal. Shocked and frightened, she awoke in a cold sweat.

When she realized she had encountered her father's ka, she immediately called to Archangel Michael to bind and remove it. She never had a repetition of the dream, and she is at peace, knowing that Archangel Michael responded swiftly to her prayer.

The astral ka may look like the person. It may also *feel* like the person who has died, since it is made up of the residual energy of their emotional body. But it is important to remember that it is *not* the person. It is merely the residual astral sheath, no longer under conscious control of the soul. The astral ka must be bound and removed by the angels of Archangel Michael in answer to our prayers so that it does not go out and cause harm to others.

Sometimes people feel as if a family member or a close friend is still nearby for some time after their passing. This is a sign that there is more spiritual work to do, and the calls need to be made to Archangel Michael and the angels for the clearing of the astral ka and for the soul to be taken to the right place for her next assignment.

Cremation of the body after death can be helpful in dealing with this problem. After a three-day period of rest in which the soul and the finer vehicles withdraw from the form, the purification by fire frees the residual energy in the body. It also helps free the soul and the finer bodies to move on to higher octaves, free of a sense of attachment to the body or the planes of earth. This is particularly important for the emotional body, which is the one most closely affinitized to the physical body.

Seduction by the Suicide Entity

Another factor that plays a part in suicide is forces of darkness known as *mass entities.* These entities are the accumulation of mankind's own momentums of hatred, violence, war, greed, envy, grief, fear, lust, gossip, and the like. These entities, as islands of darkness, float in the astral belt and are moved on the grid of the field of human consciousness by diabolical forces that direct these pools of dark power against unsuspecting lifestreams.

The mass entity associated with suicide is known as *Annihla.* Each year, thousands upon our planet exit from life by opening themselves to the despondent vibrations of the suicide entity. This force of suicide can be felt as a magnetic pull, almost like an undertow in the water that pulls the soul into the depths of depression and despair.

Souls under the influence of the suicide entity often do not know that the entity exists or that it has a name. But they feel its pull. It influences their thoughts and projects the idea of death as attractive, desirable, even heroic—the solution to their problems. People who are considering suicide usually think these are their own thoughts and feelings, but often they are merely projections. And if people start to internalize these ideas and make them their own, then these thoughts are very much amplified by the suicide entity—the mass entity, Annihla, as well as discarnate entities of suicide.

This force of the suicide entity works overtime in all large cities of the world. Sometimes it is very active in particular places, for example in San Francisco prompting people to jump off the Golden Gate Bridge. It works overtime on Wall Street during a crash in the stock market. Wherever darkness and despair are present, the suicide entity stalks, along with its agents or "tools" in embodiment, promoting its wares.

For those who are healthy—physically, mentally and emotionally—the suicide entity will not have much of an inroad. When energy is moving in a positive spiral, there is not much attraction in death. Therefore the first step is usually to try to get people involved in some seemingly "harmless" activity by which they lose or misuse their light and energy.

Use of drugs and alcohol is one way that the balance of energy is changed in the body. There is a certain damage to the physical body that occurs, and at the same time the finer bodies are also affected and light is lost from the aura. Partaking of drugs was for many who have committed suicide the first in a series of steps toward self-annihilation. The first indulgence, the first drink, the first entering in is the preliminary stage of the development of an addiction and the start of the breakdown of the energies of the primary spiritual center, the heart chakra, so that the heart might become the seat of darkness instead of light.

While the angels and the masters of light would lead the youth on a spiritual path to higher consciousness, the suicide entities that come to seduce the youth have calculated their own path—step by step lower in light and consciousness as the antithesis of the spiritual path.

Suicide Clusters and Copycat Suicide

Psychologists and experts will tell you that suicide is contagious. Suicide clusters are a well-known phenomenon, and they have been recorded even as far back as ancient Greece.

Sometimes we find these clusters occurring in families or communities. Loren Coleman, in his book *Suicide Clusters,* gives many examples of this phenomenon. One case he describes is a cluster of nine teen suicides on the Wind River Indian Reservation in Wyoming between August 12 and September 30, 1985.

Coleman quotes one official's reaction to these events: "Marjene Tower, a behavioral specialist with the Bureau of Indian Affairs, felt the suicides were 'some sort of contagion that we don't understand. I've never seen this kind of epidemic before.' Tower's most shocking discovery was the fact that all of the fourteen- to seventeen-year-old suicide victims were best friends, pall-bearers at each others' funerals. Among the young men, they were 'drinking buddies.' She felt the suicides were 'caught' like other diseases spread among closely related individuals."[5]

Unfortunately, such "epidemics" are more common than is widely known. Sometimes they follow the depiction of suicide in news reporting or even in movies. In these cases, often known as copycat suicide, the victims may be separated geographically, but they act out many of the details of the original suicide.

For example, there was a rash of suicides following the release of the film *The Deer Hunter*, which includes a scene where POWs are forced to play Russian roulette by Vietnamese Communists. Later, one of the characters in the movie becomes so distraught that he plays willingly and kills himself.

Suicide researchers Thomas Radecki and Alan Berman have documented forty-three Russian-roulette deaths worldwide in the eight years following the film's release. All of these cases were clearly linked to recent viewing of the film—some were carried out while actually watching it.[6]

In such cases, we can see, on a spiritual level, that each time another person succumbs to the pull of suicide, more energy is fed to the suicide entities on the astral plane, and another astral ka is added to the mix. Like spiritual vampires, these entities feed upon the light released from each new suicide and they use this light to perpetuate themselves. They move from one individual to another, trying to convince people that they are alone, that no one understands them and they should end it all. Yet, ironically, suicide is misery that loves company.

Counseling and intervention with psychological and emotional support can play an important part in breaking this cycle. But we also recognize the unearthly character of the force of suicide, and we know that, although it is beyond *human* remedy, there are spiritual solutions.

In response to the Wind River suicide cluster, a task force of agencies stepped in to provide counseling and support for teens and families. But as well as this, the Arapaho tribal elders held a sacred ritual that had not been used since 1918, when it was performed to ward off an outbreak of Spanish influenza. Hundreds of the community's youth stood in line to receive a spiritual cleansing performed by the tribal elder. Following this ceremony on October 7, the winter of 1985–86 was calm, with no more suicides reported on the reservation.[7]

The forces of darkness are no match for the angels and masters of light. Our task is to invite these legions of light into the battle.

The Effects of Music

Music is a major influence in all of our lives, and it can either uplift or depress the soul. It is a factor in many cases of suicide, yet it is one that is very often overlooked.

After her suicide attempt and near-death experience, Angie Fenimore had a very clear realization of the influences that had led her to suicide. She had a history of abuse as a child, as well as drug and alcohol use. Yet she saw that the music she had absorbed herself in was a key factor. In her book, *Beyond the Darkness,* she says:

"I understood that everything that enters our minds influences us and can alter the balance of light and darkness within us. Around the time of my death, I found myself attracted to morbid and dark literature as well as television and movies of a dark nature....

"At that time, almost all my clothes were black, a seemingly insignificant coincidence that was actually a clear indication of where I was headed. And probably the most significant dark influence on me was the music I listened to. Some music may have words that seem harmless—mindless, in fact—but when these words are paired with musical combinations that have a dark spiritual form, they have the power to create more darkness in the minds of those of us who hear them.

"We can 'feel' whether the tones of a particular piece are created of light or darkness by how the music reacts with our own spirit to create a mood. The music I chose at that time lulled me into a stupor, preaching death and selfishness in symbolic phrases, and it crowded out the light."[8]

It is not just the words but the rhythm of the music as well that can have a profound effect on our chakras, our spiritual centers. Music has elevated the earth into golden ages—and also contributed to the decline and destruction of great civilizations. With the advent of rock and rap music and the syncopated beat, music is changing the vibration and the inner mechanism of souls evolving on earth today. The world's acceptance of music with a negative influence has dulled spiritual perception as people have gradually become more and more used to the darkness that is present in much of the music heard today.

When you are accustomed to it, you do not even notice it;

but even worse, once you go a little bit too far into darkness, once you cross over the line, you may find that you have become "comfortable" living in the dark influences of the music. You become addicted to the beat, which is echoed by forces on the astral plane. You are in a downward spiral of energy, and you don't know where it will end. And by the time you reach the point of suicide or some other crisis, you may find that you are not able to resist the downward pull. At that point you have to implore the living God to rescue you—and seek help from friends, family, counselors, anyone who can be the instrument of that rescue.

There is much music that has been inspired by higher sources. Classical music, sacred music, folk music, waltzes, square-dance music—the kind of music that uplifts and conveys beauty and light—can raise your consciousness and soothe your soul.

We should all consider the effect of music in our worlds and especially on our chakras, which govern the flow of divine energy and connect us with our Higher Self. Then we can make choices accordingly.

Evil Forces Are the Tempters

The evil forces that inflict themselves upon people tempt them to do all kinds of things they regret. Suicide begins with the draining of the life force through anything that results in the untimely and premature release of light and energy from the chakras. This is often the extreme of heightened emotions coming through the false exhilaration of drugs, alcohol, illicit sex, rap music, rock concerts and panic-invoking horror movies.

There is a charge of energy that you feel in all of these activities, but this is the release of light as the chakras become drained. In that feeling of being drained, there is not the emotional control to resist, and there is not even physical strength to fight the forces that have arranged the plotting of one's death.

It is especially a concern when people engage in these things at younger and younger ages. Before the chakras have fully developed, when the emotional and mental bodies are still developing (as is the physical), these misuses of energy can set up patterns that can be difficult to overcome in later years.

The link between emotional or sexual abuse of children and suicide is well established. In these situations, professional counseling is essential. These children are often burdened by a great sense of guilt and unworthiness, thinking that they have somehow caused the abuse. Healing is needed at all levels of being, and understanding and working with the spiritual dimension can be an important adjunct to this healing.

We have also seen that as the age level for experiencing sexuality has dropped in recent decades, teen suicide rates have risen dramatically. People are now beginning to understand the spiritual perspective and to see what the angels clearly note from inner levels—that early teen or pre-teen sex is a factor in suicide.

Sex in itself is not a sin, nor is it wrong. Within the sacred circle and commitment of marriage, the exchange of energies between man and woman is a beautiful experience that uplifts and blesses when the energies are so consecrated. When taken outside of the bond of marriage, with multiple partners and under the influence of drugs and alcohol, sex quickly drains and lowers the energy in the spiritual centers. Teenagers emerge from these experiences looking old before their time and with a jaded outlook on love and life. Depression sets in, and a door is opened for the suicide entity.

So there we have it—the old story of drugs, sex and the syncopated beat of rock and rap music, which assault the chakras and lower the energies in the body temple—cheating children, teens and people of all ages of the light they need to fulfill their divine plan.

What If I Only Contemplate Suicide?

It is fashionable among some teens today to talk about suicide, never really intending to carry it out. But this practice may not be as harmless as it seems. Those who contemplate suicide, even though they may not initially intend to follow through or do any more than think about it, do have a tendency to attract suicide entities. The entities then work on an emotional level to make suicide seem attractive or desirable.

Also, where your thoughts and feelings are during your waking hours determines where you travel in consciousness while you sleep, and those who indulge in the idea of suicide will often gravitate to the astral plane while they sleep at night instead of going to the cities of light in the heaven-world. They are then vulnerable to the pull of suicide entities that stalk the canyons of the astral plane.

This can be a slippery, downhill slope. As the thoughts and

feelings of suicide become more and more integrated into a person's consciousness, this can lead to increased vulnerability to suicide at a later time, when unexpected sadness comes into their life or they are unable to cope with a disappointment or challenge.

Those who are most influenced by suicide entities descend in consciousness lower and lower into the astral plane, and not until it is too late do they realize that they are not able to disentangle themselves from these entities. The entities are patient. Having set their traps, they are often willing to wait a long time for the bait to work.

There is a way out of this downward spiral. But once people have gone a certain way down this road, they frequently require help to get out of the quicksand. Spiritual intercession is often essential for people to be cut free from these ties to the astral plane and the suicide entities. And prayer is the key to this intercession. For according to cosmic law, the archangels of God and their hosts may not descend into the realms of death and hell to rescue souls unless they receive an appeal from devotees of God to do so.

People caught in these traps can pray on their own behalf for the intercession of the angels. But such souls are often so burdened by their karma and so bowed down by the taunting of these demons and hellions that they no longer have the strength or the will to resist their tormentors. They no longer have any hope that their prayer might be answered or even the faith to pray. And therefore the faithful must pray to God daily and fervently that imprisoned souls might be cut free from their demon oppressors and be given another opportunity to choose God and choose life.

The Last Enemy

One of the greatest temptations that people face—those older in years or invalids, or perhaps those who are young but have been surfeited with life's pleasures—is to think that death is a doorway to bliss, to immortality, or to some experience we cannot have here. This is the lie and this is the temptation of the suicide entity. That suicide entity comes in many guises, not just in the temptation to take one's life, but in the temptation to look forward to death as somehow the surcease from pain and suffering.

But in reality, there is no sudden purification, no sudden halo of glory in the transition to another level of existence. There is no great mystery about this thing we call death. Whatever you are right now, at the moment of transition, you will still be. Thus we see the words of the Book of Revelation, "He that is filthy, let him be filthy still."

If you are pure, so that purity will be ratified in the Christ, and you will find yourself in the glory of the ascension. And if you are filthy because you have accepted the consciousness of sin concerning yourself, you will dwell in that consciousness of sin that Catholics have called purgatory and which Buddhists call *bardo*—the astral plane. You dwell in that plane until you can overcome that sense of sin and until that sense dies by the weight of its own unreality.

The more you learn of light and the spiritual path, the more that temptation is put before you. As in any temptation, it is not something that you face one day and it's forevermore gone and behind us. Temptation doesn't work that way. It comes again and again and again. It keeps knocking at the door according to cycles of the moon and cycles of your karma as you encounter the records of death.

Therefore, to remember this truth—that you cannot die, you will never die, you will only move from room to room in the consciousness of God—makes you resist that temptation of the tempter. And then in the hour when you are called home to the heart of God, it is not an experience, either for you or for your loved ones, of what people call death. It is that gentle passing of the breath of the Holy Spirit into another plane of consciousness.

People who have witnessed the passing of those who do not have light, as opposed to the passing of those who do, know the difference. They know the aura and the feeling that surrounds individuals who have been consecrated to a life of service and devotion to God and those who haven't. You can feel where the soul is and where it is lodged. And so we know there is no death. And in that knowledge, we never succumb to the "delicious magnetism" of death, the pulling of the entities of death who would taunt us in the hours of aloneness and make us enter into the spirals of what they term "the sweet sense of death." The flowing with the downward spiral is so easy; it is so easy not to fight; it is so easy to give in.

When Paul said, "I die daily," he meant that the carnal mind was being put down daily and it was being replaced by the Christ mind. But there are people all over the planet who are dying daily, and it is the Christ in them that is dying because they give way to this downward pull of energies descending on the spine, being squandered on the lusts of the flesh, spending their life's energies so that there is nothing left whereby they can enjoy the real flame of life.

We must realize, then, that this last enemy doesn't come just at the end of a lifetime. It comes daily. It comes in the temptation to self-indulgence, to moving in the pleasure cult. The pleasure cult is very real and very rampant on the planet. We see it each day as we walk through the cities of the world and see those "who toil in their merrymaking," as Gautama

Buddha says. They work so hard to have a good time. They work much harder having a good time in the pleasures of the flesh than those on a spiritual path do having a good time in the light. It's actually easier to move in the light and the consciousness of the light.

The squandering of energy, then, upon the limited pursuits of the world and the flesh is a daily dying of the Christ light in you. This is the death to be concerned about, because this is the enemy that is milking you of your flame and your light.

There are not many among mankind who, after transition, have enough light to propel themselves to the higher octaves. Most wind up on the astral plane because they have squandered that life force. And there is, then, nothing in their aura to sustain a momentum of propulsion into the higher octaves.

This is a very dangerous state to be in. And we should think about it because the years move swiftly by, and our light, which is our inheritance, can be squandered without our even realizing it. The warning to watch out for the temptation of death is always timely, because it is an initiation we all must pass.

The Cause behind the Effect of Suicide

When we are in a weakened state or our aura is depleted for any reason, we are much more likely to be susceptible to suggestions or thoughts of suicide. When the aura is not strong, we no longer have our natural defenses against the influence of the entities of depression and suicide. The problem is compounded if we are also dealing with the entities of harmful substances we are taking into the body.

Those who are depressed often turn to alcohol and drugs in a vain attempt to dull or deaden the emotional or mental pain they are experiencing. There is a temporary relief, but a vicious cycle quickly results. The loss of light in the aura as a result of alcohol or drugs triggers deeper depression, which leads to a deeper reliance on drugs. And so it progresses, step by step.

At a certain point, the suicide entity steps in to tempt the soul to make the ultimate choice of ending life in what may seem like a logical or "best" solution. This may come in the form of thoughts that are projected and may seem like the person's own. Some people report that they have even heard a "voice" saying, "Just get rid of yourself, and all of your problems will be over," or "Your family will be better off without you."

Tempting, yes; seductive, certainly. But not rooted in reality.

The problems will not be over. For they must be faced again in another embodiment—with the added karmic baggage of suicide. And if your family is already having problems, life will be so much worse if they have to cope with losing you, their loved one, as well. They will have to go on without you and deal with the pain of that loss and feelings of guilt and shame about what they might have done to prevent the tragedy.

What is this voice that urges people to suicide? Certainly it is not the voice of the Higher Self, the Good Shepherd, the inner voice of God. The voice from higher realms does not urge us to death or suicide, but always affirms life.

No, it is the voice of the "not-self," the antithesis of your Real Self, the conglomerate of all that is unreal and dark that you have ever taken in and harbored in the depths of your being. And it has a name: the *dweller-on-the-threshold*.

Energetically, that dweller is the nucleus of a vortex of energy that forms the electronic belt, shaped like a kettledrum and surrounding the four lower bodies from the waist down. Your electronic belt contains the cause, effect, record and memory of your human karma in its negative aspect. The dweller-on-the-threshold is the focal point of the consciousness behind the human creation—the mind behind the manifestation.

The term *dweller-on-the-threshold* conveys the meaning that it "dwells" or sits at the threshold of self-awareness where the elements of the subconscious cross the line from the unconscious to the conscious world of the individual, and the unknown not-self becomes the known. Once surfaced, the dweller has entered the realm of the conscious will where the soul may choose to "ensoul" or to slay the components of this antithesis of his Real Self.

It's right there ready to come through the door of consciousness, but at that threshold, at the line separating the planes of awareness, the guardian action of the Christ mind, the holy angels and one's free will stand to prevent the dweller from actually surfacing and moving into action in our world.

The Christ mind, God within us, can outwit the forces of suicide. God with you can be victorious.

Discernment Is the Key

What the false hierarchy of darkness really wants is to make you abort your mission in this life by committing spiritual suicide. And remember, these discarnate entities bent on your failure will keep playing on your weakest point until you or they win. This is a contest in which only you can decide the winner.

Discernment is the key. By their fruits we know them. The voice that urges us to go against God's laws—to commit suicide or to indulge in things that would shorten our life—is the voice of the entities on the astral plane, often working in concert with our own dweller-on-the-threshold.

C. S. Lewis once wrote a satire on the hierarchy of devils who plot the demise of aspirants on the spiritual path—with meticulous planning and cunning performance. His book, *The Screwtape Letters,* has become a classic in the field of spiritual literature. And although it seems Lewis didn't believe in the literal existence of these disembodied spirits, he was an astute student of their psychology (and of that of the Christian neophyte) and their modus operandi.

Of course, the cleverest tool of all is discouragement. They say the devil carries a little satchel and that he has one very sharp tool. People ask, "What tool is that?" Well, the devil himself will tell you, "That's discouragement." When the dark ones fail to get us through any other means, they will use the tool of discouragement every time. Sometimes they use it at the precise moment people are about to have a breakthrough or achieve their goal.

It can happen quite simply. You become disheartened by something that someone close to you does or says. You feel dejected because you're disappointed—you've pinned your faith or your love on someone, and you think they've failed you just when you needed them most.

Call to the angels, refute the voices, ask for heavenly intercession from Jesus and the saints, ask your friends and family to pray for you.

And if you are challenged by thoughts or projections of suicide, seek medical help. God often answers prayers through people in the physical. And even if they are not aware on the outer of the part they are playing in the plan, God and the angels can use their training and experience as the most practical means to deliver the intercession that has been called for.

Sometimes doctors will prescribe medication as a means to deal with depression or imbalances in the mental or emotional body. Interestingly, the medication often employed in the treatment of such disorders, when viewed from a spiritual dimension, can be seen to coat the aura, sealing it from the astral plane and keeping out the voices of the night. Although it may temporarily dull the spiritual sensitivities, when necessary, it can be life-saving.

The Choice to Live

The decision to end one's life is viewed with great sadness by the heavenly beings. Although they understand the pressures and complexities of life on earth, they also understand that to choose suicide is to fail a test that is given in the schoolroom of life.

Suicide does not contribute to the forward evolution of the soul. It is a backward step, and the soul will need to return to earth to correct the mistakes of poor choices. From the view point of the heavenly realm, the choice to take one's life is actually seen as one of the worst decisions one can make spiritually and physically—the consequences are that far-reaching.

According to cosmic law, the choice to live or die is not ours to make. We cannot decide when to end our life. We cannot say, "This is my time to leave." God is the one who decides when it is time for man, woman or child to lay down their body, according to the cosmic timetables, and move to the octaves of light.

The timetables for the soul are exact, directed by angels and masterful beings who are the sponsors of the soul—the God-parents, if you will. Archangels and cosmic beings of light direct the timetables of birth and death for every soul according to God's grand design.

It is spiritually unlawful to take your own life, no matter what the reason: whether to reach a Higher Source or to escape unpleasant circumstances. We simply can't play God.

Are There Ever Exceptions?

We can all understand the tragedy of teenagers cutting short their lives and losing the great potential that lay before them. But what about the elderly and those who suffer from incurable diseases or painful illnesses, with loss of function and quality of life?

From the perspective of the soul, life is still a gift, and it is never correct to take one's own life. No matter how difficult or painful the circumstances, suicide is not the answer.

Where there is life, there is God—imprisoned in form, perhaps, but a spark of God, nevertheless—and a temple of God is worthy of love and compassion and care. All is designed for the instruction of the soul and the growth of the Spirit in man and woman.

We have many stories of overcoming, of the triumph of the Spirit in all types of human adversity. What if deaf and blind Helen Keller or her teacher, Anne Sullivan, had given up?

What if Beethoven had accepted the silence of deafness instead of continuing to compose music? These courageous souls and others too many to list tell us that all life is sacred and is to be cherished. We also see that suffering is a part of life's experience, and sometimes it is the crucible of suffering that allows the highest potential of the soul to appear.

The courage with which many cope with chronic illness and face terminal illness is an inspiration. In many cases, these souls have agreed to balance karma in their bodies. They suffer a little while in the world that they may have, as Saint Paul says, a "better resurrection."[9] And some souls, following in the footsteps of Jesus, have volunteered to hold the balance for planetary karma in the physical body.

There are saints among us who have endured suffering and pain, burdens in their bodies, long-term illnesses, and they truly bear the light of the saints of heaven. They are working out their salvation with fear and trembling,[10] with immense pain of the body yet great joy and expectation of the soul. And they will carry on until God calls them Home. They will do everything in their power to become stronger and healthier and to get well, to have one more day in the service of God, one more day to sing his praise even in the midst of the greatest adversity.

Yes, every effort should to be made to alleviate human suffering through all available means that are lawful in God's eyes. But the key is to let events take their course (with all that man has at his disposal to help) so that God and the Higher Self may decide when and where it is time for the soul to move on to higher ground.

The story is told of an elderly woman who decided to stop eating so that she might hasten her end. This is also a manifestation of suicide. When she passed on, she went before a council of beings of light who told her in no uncertain terms that it was wrong to stop eating in order to invite death. She had interfered with the timetables of her soul.

Her physical problems were opportunities for learning love, patience and compassion for others and for the expiation and balancing of karma. This soul was going to have to spend much time in the heaven-world atoning for her ingratitude for the gift of life, and a decision would be made as to whether she would need to return to embodiment to balance that karma or could remain and serve in the heaven-world.

Love is the means by which we solve all problems. We all need love—the divine love that loves the soul just as she is and yet will not leave her as it finds her. Sometimes we need tough love—the love of a friend who will tell us our faults and how to correct them, the love of a parent who draws loving boundaries and explains why a certain behavior is not acceptable. This is the love the angels and masters give us.

Choose Life, Not Death

Jesus said, "Except ye be converted and become as little children, ye shall not enter into the kingdom of heaven."[11]

And it is true. To enter the kingdom of heaven requires childlike trust. When parents, teachers, friends and governments reject God or do not include God in life, then doubt, fear and a deep sense of loneliness and loss permeate the mind and heart. Rather than trusting in God, people begin to believe that there is no recourse, nowhere to turn, because that is what is being drummed into their mind.

Suicide breeds in a godless society; a godless home and a godless society lead the soul into despair. Many have said, "There is no God," and concluded that human life is meaningless. What, then, becomes the reason for being? Many who embraced existentialism became suicidal because they had nothing left to live for.

Suicide is the death of the body, but it can also be the

death of the soul. To repeat: Those who commit suicide, depending on their karma and the circumstances of their death, are required by the law of life either to remain on various levels of the astral plane or to immediately reincarnate.

This they must do to balance the karma they made by committing suicide and abandoning those lifestreams for whom they were responsible. Once and for all, they must learn the lesson that suicide is not a way out of one's problems and that taking one's life will not send the soul to Elysian fields, as the suicide demons promise, but back to square one—to have to do it all over again.

Often those who have committed suicide stay close to home in their astral bodies and attempt in vain to speak to family members and close friends. They try to express their regret and their profound sorrow that they have committed such a crime as to snuff out the flame of life God gave them at birth.

Yes, they know now that the crime of taking life is the ultimate crime. But why didn't they know it before? All the world's scriptures tell us that life is sacred, that life is God and that life must be embraced in its fullest potential and defended.

Even Moses counseled the children of Israel to choose life: "I have set before you life and death, blessing and cursing: therefore choose life, that both thou and thy seed may live."[12] We have the same choice to make today.

The Story of One Soul

By Elizabeth Clare Prophet

I recently read a story of a very devout young woman, Catholic, serving in her church with great joy. All of a sudden this girl mysteriously died or was killed or even perhaps committed suicide. And from the moment that I heard her name and saw this article in the newspaper in Los Angeles, my heart was gripped with a sense that here was a soul who met a crisis she could not face.

Something happened to her. Perhaps she made a mistake. Perhaps she did something that was not in her eyes equal to the life of devotion she had begun. But I wept over her death, and I felt such a great loss of such a beautiful soul of light.

One evening before I went to bed, I went outside to meditate and be at peace for a while. And I called to Mother Mary, the Queen of the Angels, for assistance for her soul. And Mother Mary showed me this particular one. She was being borne by angels, and she was wrapped in a swaddling garment of light.

The soul of this young woman appeared as it would appear in her native innocence, almost in the childhood or baby state, and yet it had the full presence of her as she was when she passed from the screen of life. I saw how she was being borne to other realms and truly cared for. And yet, I had the sense that if I had been near that young woman in the hour of her crisis, if I could have held her hand and prayed with her, that that death would not have come to pass.

It really burdened my heart. I want you to know this. And I have not ceased to be burdened by it, because I feel that the emphasis upon sin, the accusations that people face—whether from their communities or through the press or the media, the condemnation heaped upon condemnation—for many people creates a burden they are not able to bear. They are not able to bear the censure and the scorn of public opinion that agrees, according to its moral codes, that this is the unforgivable sin. Under the weight of public opinion, they take their lives or they quit helping people.

And as I am in the heart of Mother Mary this day, I feel these are the things that are on her heart and that were she to ask us a favor in this hour, it would be to pray for the alleviation of that burden of suffering of people who suffer under this censure of others.

The Mother comes to heal us all of our sense of sin regarding ourselves or other people. She comes to liberate us, especially in the Christian world, of the enormous division that renders Christianity ineffective. And of course, she comes carrying the sorrow of the people of every single nation on the planet and the determination to help them, to intercede as we give our prayers.

PART 3

APPROACHING THE PROBLEM

A Reason to Live

We all need a reason to live, a reason for being. We all need to know that we are loved. When we have the vision of our higher purpose, when we know we are loved, then we know what we are called to do and we do choose life. By the grace of God and the Holy Spirit, we can give that gift to one another and to ourselves.

Yet it is possible for anyone at any time to lose their sense of identity, purpose and reason for being, and to suddenly feel there is no longer any more reason for being alive. Periods of despair are a part of the human condition and come to all of us, whether from cycles of returning karma, fluctuations in body chemistry; events in our lives such as the loss of a loved one, an accident or illness or life-threatening condition, or any other difficult circumstance or challenge that life can send our way.

How do you distinguish between a difficult time in life, a dark night of the soul for the balancing of karma, and an entity-driven suicidal state?

First, it is important to be aware of the warning signs for suicide (see pages 192–93). But beyond this, there is the gift of discernment of spirits—one of the gifts of the Holy Spirit. Your Higher Self will lead the way, assisted by angels and beings of light. You have inner guidance and a reservoir of light that can help you. The Holy Spirit can use you to offer comfort and healing to others in the very moment they need it.

One woman's story illustrates how one person can be an instrument of the Holy Spirit in saving a life. She was awakened in the early hours of the morning, concerned for an elderly neighbor two doors down the street. The woman lay in bed for a few moments unable to get back to sleep and unable to stop thinking of her neighbor, an older woman who had recently lost her husband of many years and was in frail health.

Finally, after praying for direction, even though it was still dark, the woman went next door and discovered her neighbor trying to kill herself by placing her head in the gas oven. Fortunately, she had come just in time, prompted by her angels and her Higher Self.

It is important that we follow those promptings and intimations of the Holy Spirit. Angels can whisper to us, but we need to be ready to listen and to act.

Pursuing Your Passion

Teenagers and adults who discover and pursue their passion rarely fall prey to the suicide entity. They are too busy engaging in healthy activities and creative endeavors that build a sense of self-worth.

Passions of healthy young people take many forms: sports, drama, science, literature, music, art, dance, cheerleading, photography, service projects or starting a business—the list is almost endless. Whatever activity a young person chooses, it will be fruitful if it expands the mind, builds the body, uplifts the emotions and fulfills the hopes and dreams of the soul. The important point is that the young person is passionately interested in whatever he or she is pursuing.

Support of parents and mentors is a major factor in whether a teen is going to be successful. Teenagers often put on a show of not caring what their parents think—but that's often all it is, an act *in case* the parents really aren't interested.

Underneath a surface bravado, the young person is yearning for a pat on the back, an encouraging word and a hug for a job well done. At the same time, we have to allow them to win their own victories—to provide support but not to do it for them.

And we can't forget academics. The school years provide the basic building blocks for fulfilling the mission of life. Again, parental support and encouragement (and tutoring or other help as needed) go a long way toward helping young people maintain a positive attitude toward learning.

One of the benefits of young people following their dreams is that they learn to be self-motivated. And in the service of a project they are excited about, they will learn methods, facts, figures and skills that serve them for life. Parents and teachers can't do it for them, but they can pray for their safety and cheer them on to victory.

The Importance of a Loving Family

Many young people who commit suicide take that desperate action because they feel alone, as if they don't belong or are not part of the crowd. And the best way to prevent or heal these feelings is a strong family tie. Parents and friends of youth need to realize what an important role they play in preventing suicide.

How vital it is for young people's self-esteem to have loving parents in whom they can confide. Knowing they have a loving, supportive family gives a sense of belonging and helps a teen or young adult resist peer pressure and the enticement of dangerous or unlawful activities. A strong sense of self and family identity is one of the most powerful bulwarks against suicide.

When we see the rise of teen suicide rates in the last thirty years, we see the signs that we need to wage a concerted effort to deal with the forces of darkness on the astral plane that would try to entice a soul to commit suicide. And we need to make an effort to get involved with children, youth and families so that they will have the support they need amid the storms of life.

Most of all, we need to love the souls of our children and youth—and our own soul as well—and affirm *life* in all of its wonder and glory.

An Appeal to Loving Adults

The age of the soul is not determined by the age of the body. There are great spiritual beings in the small bodies of the children and youth of the world. Young people deserve to know love and a caring touch in their early years and in their teens. They need to be told of a loving God and the way of light and divine purpose. They have a right to enjoy abundant opportunities.

Youth are very perceptive, and they look to actions more than words. One soul recently arrived in heaven writes about teenagers: "They look for adults with joy and balance and mastery. No matter how they behave personally and no matter what they claim to want, on a soul level teens recognize the 'true parent' or the righteous adult....

"The teenage world is bombarded with unreality. If teens receive a strong foundation in Reality and balance in their earlier years, they will not forget this. It is recorded in their souls."[13]

The presence of a significant adult in the lives of children and teenagers can make all the difference in their fulfilling their potential. Yet many parents need help with the challenges that face them and their families.

There are many people who have the calling to get involved with children and youth, to help in some way, great or small. If you feel your Higher Self and the angels calling you to this, there are many things you can do—help with teen programs and youth centers, get involved with activities at your local high school, find out about your church's youth programs, or sign up with your local Big Brothers or Big Sisters program. Even just talking with young people, spending time with them and accepting them for who they are, can make a big difference.

Most adults who get involved with children and teens will tell you that they themselves are the ones who benefit from the experience, even more than the young people they serve. Being around young people reminds you of what is important in life and can help you find a joy and spontaneity that we sometimes lose as adults. It gives you the opportunity to extend love and compassion and to open your own heart and to see the opening of the heart of a child or teenager.

And don't think that you do not have anything to share or

to teach. You do! Besides passing on skills that can help young people later in life, just by being who you are, you also model how you cope with life, how you handle problems and how you apply spiritual principles in your world. Think of the tasks you do each day and the simple chores of life, and do them with children and teens. You will have more fun, and so will they.

Be a mentor. Be a friend. Be the champion of the soul and Higher Self. Spend some time each day praying for our children and youth. Ask God to send to the children and youth the teachers and mentors who can help them—and don't be surprised to find that you are one of them!

Do not ignore the little child or the teenager that God sends to your door. Making a difference in the life of one child or teen can be the boost they need to make it through life's challenges—and the boost you need toward the fulfillment of your own divine plan.

Jesus gave the example: "Suffer the little children to come unto me." Truly, as he said, "If you have done it to the least of these my brethren, ye have done it unto me."[14]

Teen Mentors and Peer Support Groups

Many high schools have developed mentor and peer support programs, and these programs can be very effective in helping teens navigate through the challenges of these years.

In mentor programs, older students provide young people from grade school or junior high friendship and support. One-on-one help from someone a bit older and more experienced in handling challenges similar to yours can help change your perspective on difficult issues. And when your perspective shifts, you tend to think of new possibilities. When you try new possibilities, you gain more experience.

You win some; you lose some—but with the guidance of a mentor added, the result is typically a gain in self-confidence and an ability to meet challenges more successfully. These programs have kept many a young person out of trouble and on track, both in school and outside activities.

Peer support programs are another excellent avenue for

providing a support structure for teens and helping them deal positively with the challenges of life. These programs may be as simple as groups of students getting together once a week to share and support each other. Often, just knowing you have peers with whom you can share your hopes, dreams and challenges makes a big difference.

As one young girl put it, “I look forward to my peer group meetings. I can go to my group and talk about whatever is bothering me. And a lot of times I find out that the other girls have felt the same way I do. That helps me a lot. Plus, it’s getting easier for me to share my feelings. And I feel good about how we support each other.”

A teenage boy said, “Our peer group does sports together, like shooting baskets, hiking, snow-boarding, whatever we’re in the mood for—and then we rap about whatever is bothering us. After we work off some of the energy, we’re more ready to talk. Sometimes things seem to work out while we’re doing sports—it’s like we loosen up, and that helps. Afterwards we talk things over and support each other’s ideas. And life isn’t gloomy anymore.”

Spiritual Support Is Key

Parents, families, peers and other adults can provide teens with social and emotional support, and this in itself can be a great protection against the hopelessness and disconnectedness that is often the precursor to suicide. But spiritual support is also a key factor when dealing with the equation of suicide.

The teenage years are a time when young people are exploring their hopes and dreams, and they are also a time when the spiritual yearnings of the soul begin to unfold. These may be expressed in a desire to make a formal commitment to a church or a structured religious activity, or they may be seen simply as a desire to understand life and its purpose and their reason for being. It is important for teens to have a place where they can feel comfortable discussing and sharing these spiritual yearnings. Schools are often not a place where teens can talk openly about spiritual things, and churches can play a very important role in providing such an environment.

Youth groups and teen retreats sponsored by churches and other organizations can also help to provide the spiritual and emotional support that young people need. As one young person put it, "It's such a relief to be who I am and not have to worry about someone making fun of me for being spiritual. When I'm with my youth group or on one of our retreats, I can be real about what matters to me. It's neat to hang out with people who have the same values I do—instead of being thought of as weird. And I'm getting better at being who I really am in other situations, too."

Youth groups run by churches and service organizations can also provide a framework for service projects. Working with others to complete a project helps teens have a sense of belonging and a connection with others. And by making a difference in the lives of other people, teens gain a sense that their life is valuable to others. Many a young person has regained a sense of optimism by practicing his faith with his peers and in daily life—and feeling the uplift that comes from being true to his Higher Self.

Communication

Sometimes hopelessness and depression can arise from causes as simple as misunderstandings and miscommunication between people. In many cases, just being able to talk about a problem can bring a new perspective, and sometimes having a third party step in as a facilitator can be valuable.

Susie and her friend Grace were working on a creative art project that was really important to Susie, and she was excited about sharing her ideas. But the more she gave her input, the more Grace seemed to lose interest. One day she told Susie she didn't have any more time to be involved in the project.

Susie felt disheartened because her friend had lost interest and worried that maybe her ideas weren't that great. And she felt personally betrayed because Grace had quit the project.

As she brooded on this hurtful experience, Susie became more and more dejected because she was so disappointed. She had pinned her faith on a person she loved and trusted. And she couldn't understand why Grace had lost interest just when she needed her most. She started wondering, "What's wrong with me?"

As is true for many young people who feel rejected, Susie found herself having trouble sleeping and at times escaping into excessive sleep. She avoided Grace because she was so uncomfortable with what had happened. And she began to lose interest in her art project.

These are signs of unresolved inner conflict that can begin when you feel let down by someone you trust. The more you brood about it, the more discouraged you feel. And you even begin to think to yourself, "What's it all worth anyway, when even the people you trust let you down?"

And if you don't watch out, depression can set in, and then, when subconscious (or conscious) anger gets stirred in, you've got a potent mixture. The entities of suicide and depression can ride in on this situation and deliberately project thoughts of hopelessness when you are feeling most hurt and vulnerable. And things can eventually escalate to a nervous breakdown or a tendency to self-destruction and suicide—even when the original cause of the problem was seemingly insignificant.

In Susie's case, the school counselor intervened. She had noticed that Susie was no longer her excited, bubbly self and that she and Grace were no longer spending time together. Grace, too, seemed glum.

The counselor brought them together and helped them talk through what had happened. It turned out that Grace had felt somewhat overwhelmed by the project and thought Susie was much better at it than she was. So she withdrew and then felt terrible because Susie seemed to be avoiding her.

On Susie's part, she had been too hurt by what she saw as her friend's disinterest to approach Grace on her own, and she had lost confidence in her own creative ability.

As the counselor helped the two of them talk things through, they began to realize that they had unintentionally sabotaged their friendship by not being honest with each other. Susie had no idea that Grace was intimidated by her creative streak, and Grace had felt embarrassed to explain why she wanted to withdraw from the project.

The girls laughed and cried when they realized they had almost lost their friendship by not being honest with each other. At the end of the session with the counselor, they hugged each other and agreed that they would talk things out in the future.

Susie completed her creative art project, which earned her an A in art class. Grace took up photography, in which she had interest and talent. And they supported and championed one another's projects. As they told the school counselor when they thanked her for her help, "We've been friends forever, but we've found out we don't have to be identical twins!"

The Healing Power of Forgiveness

Forgiveness plays an important role in everyone's life. Along life's way, we have the opportunity to forgive and to trust in the purity of each heart we encounter. We can trust in the God who is the reality of the person. And that is the way we can live with the imperfections of our family members, our friends, our acquaintances, ourselves. Lacking the quality of mercy, we find that there are people who can't even live with themselves because they can't face their imperfections.

We see one form of this in the Orient, where it is not uncommon to hear of situations where a man's honor is compromised and a failure is exposed to friends, neighbors and country. He then must immediately commit suicide, hara-kiri, because he cannot live with his own dishonor.

We find the same thing in the West as well. With news instantly available all over the world, condemnation comes in landslides, and many people find they are not able to bear public censure and scorn. They think they have committed an unforgivable sin. Under the weight of public criticism, they resign from their jobs. They resign from public life. They take their lives.

Whether a public figure facing the weight of public criticism, or just a person who feels they have failed family or friends, for some, this is the trigger to ending their life. They cannot seem to ask for forgiveness or say to family, friends or the world: "I made a mistake. I've learned from it. And I will do better." Death somehow becomes an easier choice than to forgive oneself or accept forgiveness from others. This is a sad condition, and the angels surely weep.

Forgiveness is also an essential ingredient in the aftermath of suicide. Along with sadness and grief at the loss of a loved one, there may also be a thread of anger, "How could you do this to me!" We need to be able to forgive someone who has committed or attempted suicide—for abandoning us, for doing something foolish, whatever might trigger some anger or resentment.

There is also the guilt to deal with, "If only I had done something different, maybe he would not have killed himself." And so we need to be able to forgive ourselves.

Forgiveness is often a process, rather than a one-time event. We forgive, and then another pocket of resentment or anger may come to the surface. And as we surrender each layer into the flame of forgiveness, then we can find a deep peace and resolution.

As a part of the body of God on earth, we are all connected. We all need forgiveness as a habit in our lives, forgiveness for others and for ourselves. Forgiveness is a powerful means of healing, but the person we often find hardest to forgive is ourselves.

PART 4

SPIRITUAL SOLUTIONS

Divine Solutions

What is the divine solution to the problem of suicide? It does not involve blame and shame but love and compassion to all life, especially those who are burdened or bowed down with life's challenges.

Having done all that we can do to provide emotional support, a strong family and community environment, counseling and other resources, we find that there is a further dimension where the struggle continues—the realm of Spirit. And ultimately the battle of life and death (or light and darkness, good and evil) is played out in that realm. Thus, the divine solution to suicide begins with the knowledge of cosmic law.

People of all nations, especially the children and youth, need to understand that suicide is not a solution or a way out. From the spiritual realm, it is very clear—suicide only makes things worse. As we have said before, a person who commits suicide must reembody to face again the same circumstances that seemed so overwhelming.

If you are thinking about suicide because you think your life is difficult now, just imagine yourself as an infant back in the high chair again, with oatmeal dripping down your chin, waiting to grow up to face the same situation years later. It is not worth it, and suicide is never an answer. Far better to deal with life now, as bad as it may seem. There is always a way to improve the situation, maybe just one step at a time. But things will only become a lot worse by adding the karma of suicide to the equation.

The Power of Prayer

Prayer and spiritual work are another key part of the divine solution to suicide. Very often it is the unseen forces—the suicide entity and the discarnates that prowl with it—that are a primary driving force behind suicide. People become vulnerable to these forces through difficult circumstances in their lives, but if they were free from the aggressive mental suggestion of the dark ones, they might well seek more positive solutions to their problems.

Fortunately, there are unseen forces of light as well—angels, masters, cosmic beings, all waiting to help. What they are waiting for is the call, the prayer, the mantra.

We have two great gifts from the Father: life and free will. We have been given life on this planet as the bounds of our experiment in free will. What we make of things here is up to us, and part of the gift of free will is that God and the heavenly beings do not step into this realm unless we ask them to.

Prayer, meditation, mantras, decrees—these open the door between the realms of heaven and the realms of earth. And we should pray daily for the victory of our children and youth. Young and old need to pray every day for the angels to shield everyone, especially children, teenagers and young adults, from the world momentum of suicide.

We cannot pray enough for their future. They must be saved from the forces that would bring them down. So many young people are confused, angry and lacking in hope or clear values. And this should not be.

Children have angelic sponsors at inner levels who are waiting to be called upon. Pray to them, to the sponsors of youth and to every angel and master who works with them to guide, guard and protect each child and young person on earth.

The following prayer for the children and youth of the world can be given three times or more each day. Give it each morning on awakening, or at night when you go to bed, or morning, noon and night, if you prefer. You will soon have it memorized.

In fact, won't you give it right now softly or silently or out loud wherever you are, for our dear children and youth?

Protect our Youth

Beloved heavenly Father!
Beloved heavenly Father!
Beloved heavenly Father!
Take command of our youth today
Blaze through them opportunity's ray
Release perfection's mighty power
Amplify cosmic intelligence each hour
Protect, defend their God-design
Intensify intent divine

I AM, I AM, I AM
The power of infinite light
Blazing through our youth
Releasing cosmic proof
Acceptable and right
The full power of cosmic light
To every child and child-man
In America and the world!
Beloved I AM! Beloved I AM! Beloved I AM!

We also need to pray for those who have passed from the screen of life through suicide, that they may be taken to temples of light for further instruction in their spiritual evolution and that they find homes and parents who will receive them, love and care for them, and help them win their victory over suicide in the next round.

Of course, if you know someone who is suicidal, it is imperative to take steps to get needed physical help and counseling intervention. The spiritual work can proceed side by side with these things and can be an invaluable adjunct to the professional help that is very much needed. There are many who have been saved from suicide by the power of prayer when counseling and other forms of support alone would not have been sufficient.

Archangel Michael, the Angel of Protection

Archangel Michael, the mighty angel who is known as the Prince of the Archangels, goes forth into all dimensions of the world with his legions of blue-lightning angels to protect the souls of light. Michael has fashioned a sword of blue flame from pure light substance to cut people free from astral entanglements.

While this great archangel protects all lightbearers, he has a specific assignment to protect families, parents and children. He can do this more effectively if we ask for his assistance, for Archangel Michael respects free will. Like all angels, he obeys the cosmic law that says that angels can enter our lives only when they are invited.

It was Michael and his blue-lightning angels who rescued Miguel from the astral plane. A simple prayer will invite Lord Michael and his legions of blue-lightning angels into your life and the lives of your loved ones and all members of the family of God on earth. You can compose your own prayer, or simply say:

Archangel Michael, in the name of my Higher Self, I ask for the protection of my family and friends this day.

I pray for ___[insert the name of the one who is suicidal]___ *this day. Protect* ____________ *from feelings of depression and despair and anything that would make* ____________ *want to take his/her life. I ask you to please protect* ____________ *from the suicide entity, Annihla, and the projection that death is the only way to solve their problems.*

And I ask your blue-lightning angels to find the souls who are caught on the astral plane and take them to the right level of the heaven-world for their forward evolution.

[Add your personal prayers and tell Archangel Michael about any problems that may be a burden to you.]

I leave all in your hands and keeping. Thank you for hearing my prayer. According to God's holy will, I ask that this be done.

Amen.

The following mantra for protection is also powerful, especially if accompanied by visualizing a blue-flame angel above yourself or the loved ones for whom you are praying:

Lord Michael before,
Lord Michael behind,
Lord Michael to the right,
Lord Michael to the left,
Lord Michael above,
Lord Michael below,
Lord Michael, Lord Michael wherever I go!

I AM his love protecting here!
I AM his love protecting here!
I AM his love protecting here!

You can memorize this prayer and use it as a mantra, giving it three times, nine times, or as many times as you wish. Give it when you get up, as part of your daily prayers—even while you are walking the dog or driving your car. The more you give it, the more you open the door to Archangel Michael to enter in to your life and the lives of those around you.

And no matter how busy you are, or if you are suddenly in need of assistance, you can always stop and say:

"Archangel Michael, help me! help me! help me!"

This great archangel will answer immediately.

Another way we can invoke the intercession of Archangel Michael is by giving the prayer Pope Leo XIII wrote to him.

One day as Pope Leo had finished Mass, he stopped at the altar as if in a trance. Later he explained he had overheard Satan speaking to Jesus.

In a guttural, prideful voice, Satan boasted that he could destroy the Church but he needed seventy-five years to do it. The Lord replied, "You have the time; you have the power. Do what you will." The pope understood that through prayer, sacrifice and living good lives, we could offset the power of the devil and his human agents. He recognized that Archangel Michael had a great role to play in the outcome of this conflict.

So the pope composed a prayer to invoke Archangel Michael's intercession to overcome the wiles of Satan. Catholics recited this prayer at the conclusion of Mass starting in 1886, but this practice was discontinued in 1964, when Vatican II revised the liturgy.

This prayer is an updated version of Pope Leo's prayer that you can apply to any number of situations where you need the extraordinary assistance of this archangel—when your household is being torn apart by alcoholism, when someone you know is being abused or destroyed by drugs, when unseen forces move against your family, your business, your livelihood, your country—and when dealing with the forces of darkness behind suicide.

There is a blank line in the middle of this decree where you can state the burdens on your heart. Turn them over to Archangel Michael.

Saint Michael the Archangel, Defend Us in Armageddon

Saint Michael the Archangel, defend us in Armageddon, be our protection against the wickedness and snares of the devil; may God rebuke him, we humbly pray; and do thou, O Prince of the heavenly host, by the power of God, bind the forces of Death and Hell, the seed of Satan, the false hierarchy of Antichrist, and all evil spirits who wander through the world for the ruin of souls, and remand them to the Court of the Sacred Fire for their Final Judgment including ____________

____________[insert your personal prayers here]__________.

Cast out the dark ones and their darkness, the evildoers and their evil words and works, cause, effect, record and memory, into the lake of sacred fire "prepared for the devil and his angels."

In the name of the Father, the Son, the Holy Spirit and the Mother, Amen.

It Is the Angels' Role to Challenge Evil

Archangel Michael and his legions are the ones we can call on to deal with the unseen forces of darkness behind suicide. These malevolent spirits can range from discarnate entities of various types, to the mass entity of suicide, all the way to the highest fallen angels who serve under Lucifer, Satan, Beelzebub and other unnamed chieftains of the hosts of darkness.

When dealing with embodied and disembodied evil, it is important to remember that it is not our role to confront them personally. It is our job to make the call.

The reason that we don't challenge the dark forces on our own is that many of the beings of darkness have greater attainment in the misuse of God's light, energy and consciousness than we have attainment in the right use of God's light, energy and consciousness.

And while we are great spiritual beings in our God

Presence and our point of origin in God, by our misuse of that energy and our karma, we no longer have the complete and instantaneous access to that light and attainment. Therefore, we need an advocate before the Father—God the Father and the Father's light with us as our own I AM Presence.

God gave to us, each one, a Holy Christ Self, or Higher Self, as that mediator, and he sent Jesus Christ, our Lord and Saviour, to represent that Christ to us until we should be fully one with our own Christ Self. And so, if we are going to ask the angels to cast out entities or evil spirits, we always ask in the name of the Christ, in the name of Jesus, saying:

"In the name of my mighty I AM Presence and Holy Christ Self, in the name Jesus Christ, I call to Archangel Michael and the legions of angels to bind and cast out the suicide entity, Annihla, and all entities of depression or suicide that may be burdening ______[insert the name of the individual]______*."*

However, before you even make that call, you must invoke the assistance of Archangel Michael and his sword of blue flame, which he wields for our protection against the forces of evil. Make your protection secure in the presence of Archangel Michael with you through giving the prayers to this blessed archangel in the previous section or other prayers to him. You and I are no direct match for the devils or the fallen angels.

But Archangel Michael is.

This is the principle of our spiritual work in dealing with forces of darkness. **You must never challenge evil spirits on your own.** The heavenly hosts and armies of the Lord will come to your defense. They answer your call and respond to the prayers that you give. It is their job to take on the entities and forces of darkness. It is your job to make the call.

It is like picking up the phone and calling the "heavenly hotline"—hand it over to the angels, be at peace and take the practical steps to deal with the situation.*

* For additional prayers to Archangel Michael, see *Prayers, Meditations, Dynamic Decrees for the Coming Revolution in Higher Consciousness* and *Archangel Michael's Rosary for Armageddon,* published by The Summit Lighthouse.

Suicide and Terrorism

We can extend this spiritual action to help the whole world by making the call to Archangel Michael and his legions to stop the forces of suicide that work through terrorism. In recent years we have seen a rising trend where the aim of terrorists is not just to kill others, but also to kill themselves in the process. These deluded souls have been taught that by ending their lives in this way they will somehow arrive in paradise. They are either indoctrinated by their superiors or fool themselves into believing that by doing evil, they are doing a service for Allah.

The truth is that "doing evil that good may come" is the lie of the fallen angels that has been the downfall of many a soul. Only when the suicide terrorist finds himself on the astral plane will he possibly realize his error. And now it's too late. Evil has had its day. Karma has been made. And the soul of the terrorist must pay the price.

As Shakespeare put it, "To be, or not to be, that is the question." And the soul of the terrorist on the astral plane has chosen "not to be." No glorious heaven or heavenly maidens await the suicide bombers—only the dull droning of lost souls, lost through their own choices, foolishly made.

We can daily ask Archangel Michael to bind the forces of darkness behind terrorism, including the suicide entity.

A Cylinder of Protection

We all need to develop invulnerability to the forces of darkness that lurk both inside and outside our psyche and aura. And there are spiritual tools to help us.

You have access to a dazzling cylinder of white light to protect you from negative forcefields and momentums of darkness. This brilliant white-fire shield is called the "tube of light." It comes from your own Higher Self and can be a powerful forcefield of protection.

Look through God's eyes and see this beautiful pillar of white light radiating down from your own beloved God Presence and Higher Self. It helps if you visualize it as a cylinder of white fire, nine feet in diameter, extending from above you to beneath your feet, and sealed all around on the outside in a shield of blue-fire protection from Archangel Michael. (The tube of light is shown in the Chart of Your Divine Self on page 84.)

Some see themselves standing in a waterfall of light, or in a white mist that gradually solidifies to become a protective wall of white crystal surrounding them. Others use the analogy of standing within a giant milk bottle, with white light all around. Whatever thoughtform you use, when you call it forth from your Higher Self, the tube of light from the heaven-realm provides an invulnerability against the forces of darkness.

You may need to renew that forcefield of protection several times a day. Discord will shatter the forcefield of this "crystal fire mist solidified." It can rupture when you engage in inharmony of any kind, including self-pity and self-condemnation, emotional outbursts or unkind words.

If this happens, recognize it. Stop and call upon the law of forgiveness and reestablish your harmony. Then ask for the tube of light to be reestablished in your world.

Here is a short prayer to call for your own tube of light.

Tube of Light

Beloved I AM Presence bright,
Round me seal your tube of light
From ascended master flame
Called forth now in God's own name.
Let it keep my temple free
From all discord sent to me.

I AM calling forth violet fire
To blaze and transmute all desire,
Keeping on in freedom's name
Till I AM one with the violet flame.

How to Overcome the Not-Self

As well as forces of darkness from without that influence people to suicide, there is also the force of darkness from within. The not-self, or the dweller-on-the-threshold, must also be bound so that the individual can be free to follow the promptings of the Higher Self. Archangel Michael and his legions know exactly how to handle that dweller. We can call to them to bind the dweller and free someone else or free us to be who we really are.

If you are dealing with depression or thoughts of suicide, you can shout, "Archangel Michael, help me, help me, help me! Bind that dweller! Free my soul! I choose life!" That mighty archangel will answer your call. He and his angels will do their part, but the rest is up to you. Now you must choose to outwit your karmic circumstances and to give your life a positive, upward spin.

First of all, ask the angels to help you be true to your

Higher Self. Make it a point to cultivate a positive attitude, no matter what may be going on in your life. If you get stuck, ask for help from family or friends. If you start getting depressed again, tell your family and get professional help from your doctor, minister, psychologist or youth counselor. The important thing is to get unstuck as fast as possible and get yourself moving in a positive direction. With the help of family and professionals, hand-in-hand with your Higher Self, you can outsmart the dark forces.

The Comfort of the Violet Flame

Another spiritual tool in dealing with suicide is the use of the violet flame. In the heaven-world, the angels often bathe the soul in violet flame when she has been through a traumatic experience. The vibrational and transmutative qualities of that violet flame are healing and specific to each soul who receives it.

The violet flame is a high-frequency spiritual energy that can be used to smooth the rough spots in relationships and in life's challenges. This vibrant spiritual energy revitalizes and invigorates the soul as well as the physical, emotional, mental and etheric bodies, which are vehicles for the expression of the soul.

In answer to your prayers and affirmations, the angels will stand in your aura, their arms outstretched, directing violet light and energy into your consciousness, being and world. The light penetrates the atoms and cells of the body and rises up as a flame, "burning" the density of negative karma and burdens of thought and feeling.

Many people have had powerful healing experiences with the violet flame. It can be directed into the lives of those who are burdened with thoughts of suicide. This energy changes negative thoughts into positive ones and dissolves the karma from past-life experiences that might promote thoughts of suicide. It can also be used to help heal the souls of those who have passed on through suicide or other means, and to bring comfort to friends and loved ones left behind.

The violet flame is heaven's gift to all who seek to connect with the heaven-world in the Aquarian age. As we visualize a brilliant burst of violet light enfolding us, we may well see many burdens disappearing. We can think of the violet flame as the cosmic eraser, rubbing out the debts on our karmic ledger and turning darkness into light.

As you give the following simple affirmation many times a day, let it echo through your mind over and over again, until you actually see your troubles dissolving in the magical action of the violet transmuting flame:

I AM a being of violet fire,
I AM the purity God desires.

Here is another violet-flame affirmation. As you give it with the power of the spoken Word, it becomes a decree for God's light to surround you with the healing and transmutation of the violet flame.

I AM the violet flame
    In action in me now
I AM the violet flame
    To light alone I bow
I AM the violet flame
    In mighty cosmic power
I AM the light of God
    Shining every hour
I AM the violet flame
    Blazing like a sun
I AM God's sacred power
    Freeing every one

The following mantra calls for the flame of forgiveness, which is in itself a quality of the violet flame. Give this decree and imagine the action of violet flames going into all hardness of heart, all resentment and anger, all non-resolution within yourself or with others.

I AM forgiveness acting here,
Casting out all doubt and fear,
Setting men forever free
With wings of cosmic victory.

I AM calling in full power
For forgiveness every hour;
To all life in every place
I flood forth forgiving grace.

Pray for Those Who Have Committed Suicide

Prayer can have a powerful action in helping people deal with the forces of suicide. But we can also pray fervently for those who have committed suicide.

We can call to the angels to find these souls, wherever they may be caught in the astral plane, and bring them understanding of the spiritual equation, of the tests they faced, and how they can face and overcome them in the future. This prayer alone can make a big difference in the life of a soul.

We can also ask that when they return to earth, they arrive in a home where parents are strong enough to give them a good background from childhood through the teenage years and beyond.

Families Left Behind

As we see the saints striving, walking their path to God even though they must experience physical pain, we can see that in many cases, suicide is rooted in self-concern that ignores the pain that will be inflicted on loved ones.

Suicide exacts a heavy toll on those who are left in its wake. Families left behind are also victims of suicide. There is probably no greater pain than that of a father or mother whose son or daughter has exited life through suicide. There is often a sense of guilt or shame and the awkwardness of trying to explain why a loved one chose to take his or her life.

Those affected by the death of a loved one by suicide need help. There seem to be so many loose ends. Death seems so final—no chance to talk or say goodbye, no opportunity to say those things we would like to say.

For those who believe in heaven and hope that their loved one is there, pain still gnaws at the soul. No matter how many years pass, the pain won't be forgotten. The question of whether the suicide could have been prevented, the "if onlys," will always linger.

In some cases, we may be aware that there were steps that could have been taken. But sometimes there is very little warning.

It may be of some help to know that loved ones who have committed suicide are often sad beyond belief when they see the grief they have caused. They come to see that their family loved them and were doing the best they could. Their parents were human and made mistakes, but they gave their children birth and opportunity and fed and clothed them. From beyond the veil, remorseful souls try to contact their families, apologizing for the pain and grief they have caused.

Both families and the departed need comfort. It is important to forgive the one whose life has been cut off. While they may have caused great pain to themselves and to others, they are also a victim, often of forces and circumstances they were not fully aware of.

It is also important that those who are left to grieve are able to forgive themselves. Suicide in the family is very painful, and it does not help to burden ourselves with an inordinate sense of guilt. Ultimately, the soul has free will, and all of heaven will not interfere with free will. God, as a loving parent, would surely have wished to avert the suicide, even as the earthly parent would have done the same. And yet the soul made a choice and now must live with the consequences.

Prayer can achieve much. You can pray for the soul of a loved one, asking for that one be taken to temples of light to learn the lessons of life. You can speak to that one as though he or she hears you, for the Higher Self of that one will know and will deliver the message.

Writing a letter to your loved one is a powerful way of achieving inner resolution. Find a quiet place where you will not be disturbed, light a candle if you can, say a prayer, take out a clean sheet of paper and write a heartfelt letter. When you complete the letter, burn it and ask the angels to take it to realms of light where the Higher Self of your loved one dwells.

We can also pray that victims of suicide are sent in their next embodiment to families who will love them and teach them what they need to know. We can also offer to help teenagers and others who are facing the problem of suicide. Losing ourselves in service can be healing.

And for those of us who must stand at the foot of the cross while families are going through this painful experience, we can provide spiritual support and prayer work as well as help in practical ways—taking care of the other children, providing meals or doing laundry, offering a listening ear and a comforting heart.

A Wake-Up Call

Suicide rates among the youth have been rising for decades. It is time for the youth of America and the world to wake up! Seek protection from making that choice for suicide by asking the angels to bind the suicide entity. Call to the angels to clear the discarnates of those who have already committed suicide and wander about attempting to make other people join them.

When there has been a rash of suicides or when someone you know is despondent and tending toward suicide, make these calls and see the angels move in to bind the forces of darkness.

The solution is a spiritual one. The power of prayer through the Science of the Spoken Word can clear the places where the suicide entities live and work. The prayer to Saint Michael the archangel is a prayer of exorcism, but it must be used by those on earth.

Warning Signs

It is important to be able to recognize some of the common signs associated with suicide. If you see these signs in yourself or in another person, then it is essential to seek assistance.

Signs of a tendency to suicide can be subtle or obvious. Changes in sleep or eating or behavior patterns can be clues. Depression or despondency may be present. Self-destructive habits or impulsive acting-out can also be indicators. There may be emotional turmoil or feelings of hopelessness and guilt. Talking about suicide is an indicator that you can't ignore.

Previous suicide attempts and poor family relationships indicate a higher risk, as does evidence of preparation for death or specific plans for suicide. A loss within the last three to six months—such as divorce, a death of a close friend or family member or loss of a job—is often associated with a higher risk. Suicides can also occur in the period of improvement after a loss, when the person has overcome the initial shock and is now able to put thoughts of suicide into action.

Beware also of the calm before the storm. Sometimes people will feel at peace once they have made the decision to commit suicide. They have made their plans, and now all they have to do is carry them out. Previously, they were tormented, goaded by the forces of darkness that were working on them, but now they have a sense of quietness, of calm. It is a false peace. The entity has gained a commitment and has now left them alone, once the decision has been made.

If You or a Friend or Loved One Are Suicidal

If you are dealing with thoughts of suicide, please, get help right away. Call a loved one or a friend or a co-worker, or find your way to someone who can help you. Dial the Suicide Hotline: 1-800-SUICIDE, 1-800-784-2433.

Affirm life, and do your spiritual homework. Pray and ask for help from the angels. Ask others to pray for you. And remember that you have to do your part, too. You have to affirm life, reject death and keep on keeping on. Yes, it takes effort and striving. But you can do it!

The only way you can fail is if you stop trying. The masters of light will tell you that it doesn't matter how many times you fall down, just be sure you get up one more time than you fall. And the only way an angel can pick you up is if you raise yourself. Remember that, because it's crucial. People commit suicide because they refuse to pick themselves up one more time.

Remember always that God loves you. You are a beautiful soul of light. You have a Higher Self and a guardian angel who loves you, too. God has a plan for you—it may not be clear right now, but it will be in the fullness of time. All you are required to do is to take the next best step. God wants you to be in embodiment to learn the lessons of love that life can teach you. Have the courage to pass your tests, and pray for the courage and assistance to meet them.

God often shows his love through others. Be willing to accept their love and assistance. And when you have your victory, be sure to return to life in ways small and great the assistance that you have received.

If you are reading this book and have thoughts or feelings or plans for suicide or know someone who does, put down this book, and get help right away!

Death Is Not Real

In reality, there is no such thing as death. When we lay down the body, we do not die. Our soul and our spirit live on. The body is just a house, a temple for the spirit. If the near-death experience teaches us anything, it is the unreality of death and the Reality of the continuity of the soul. The masterful beings of light who have overcome and returned to heaven are also witness to the fact that death is not real. They have graduated from earth's schoolroom, and your soul wants to do the same.

In reality, your soul wants to live—not just in the finite sense of this earthly existence, but in the infinite sense of the Reality of the great spiritual being that you are at inner levels.

Notes

1. Statistics for suicide quoted in this section are from the following sources: World Health Organization (www.who.int/mental_health); Befrienders International (www.befrienders.org.suicide/stastics.htm); The Centers for Disease Control, "Suicide Prevention Fact Sheet" (www.cdc.gov/ncips/factsheets.suifacts.htm). Figures are for the year 2000 unless otherwise noted.
2. Loren Coleman, *Suicide Clusters* (Boston: Faber and Faber, 1987), p. 1.
3. Gal. 6:7.
4. John 16:33
5. Loren Coleman, *Suicide Clusters*, p. 72.
6. Ibid., pp. 98–99.
7. Ibid., pp. 72–73.
8. Angie Fenimore, *Beyond the Darkness: My Near-Death Journey to the Edge of Hell and Back* (New York: Bantam Books, 1996), pp. 137, 138.
9. Heb. 11:35.
10. Phil. 2:12.
11. Matt. 18:3.
12. Deut. 30:19.
13. Patricia Kirmond, *Messages from Heaven: Amazing Insights on Life After Death, Life's Purpose and Earth's Future* (Corwin Springs, Mont.: Summit University Press, 1999), p. 135.
14. Mark 10:14; Matt. 25:40.

Additional Resources

Books and audio recordings listed here are published by Summit University Press unless noted otherwise.

Spiritual Tools:

Books by Elizabeth Clare Prophet:

Violet Flame to Heal Body, Mind and Soul
The Creative Power of Sound: Affirmations to Create, Heal and Transform
Access the Power of Your Higher Self
How to Work With Angels
Your Seven Energy Centers: A Holistic Approach to Physical, Emotional and Spiritual Vitality
The Art of Practical Spirituality: How to Bring More Passion, Creativity and Balance into Everyday Life
Keys to the Kingdom

Other recommended books:

The Screwtape Letters, by C. S. Lewis (HarperSanFrancisco, 2001)

Death and the Afterlife:

Messages from Heaven, by Patricia Kirmond

Children's Past Lives: How Past Life Memories Affect Your Child, by Carol Bowman (Bantam Books, 1998)

Beyond the Darkness: My Near-Death Journey to the Edge of Hell and Back, by Angie Fenimore (Bantam Books, 1996). This book is unfortunately out of print at the time of writing (2003), but it can be found through on-line used-book sources such as www.amazon.com and www.abebooks.com.

Developing Your Child's Spirituality:

Nurturing Your Baby's Soul: A Spiritual Guide for Expectant Parents, by Elizabeth Clare Prophet, comp. and ed. by Nancy Hearn and Dr. Joye Bennett

The Freedom of the Child, audio recording by Elizabeth Clare Prophet

The Effects of Music:

The Science of Rhythm for the Mastery of the Sacred Energies of Life, audio recording by Elizabeth Clare Prophet

Suicide Crisis Counseling:

National Suicide Hotline
1-800-SUICIDE (784-2433)
www.hopeline.com

Covenant House
Counseling and resources for teens and adolescents
1-800-999-9999
www.covenanthouse.org

Most local communities have many resources for suicide prevention and counseling. Check the front pages of your phone book, or call 411 or 0 and ask for:

- suicide prevention
- crisis intervention
- hotlines – crisis or suicide
- community crisis center
- county mental health center
- hospital mental health clinic

Or, call 911 and ask for help. Tell them you are in danger of committing suicide.

Acknowledgments

The concepts and ideas presented in this book are a distillation of the teachings of Elizabeth Clare Prophet on the subject of suicide, combined with the fruit of our own professional experience in counseling and dealing with this issue.

For over thirty years Elizabeth Clare Prophet has given a spiritual perspective on suicide and life after death, and the spiritual concepts in this book are entirely hers. In many places, we have included her words directly. In some places we have expressed these concepts in our own words while trying to present them as accurately as possible.

For ease of reading, we have not included the large number of quote marks and endnotes that would have been required to document the original sources for all this material. If you would like to find out more about Mrs. Prophet's teaching on these and other subjects, a good place to start is the resources included at the back of the book.

Our contribution to this book has been simply to weave the threads to make the whole, to add case studies, and to provide some insight into some of the more practical aspects of dealing with suicide.

Many people from all over the world have been touched by Mrs. Prophet's teachings on this subject. We hope that you, the reader, have also gained a new perspective on the gift of life.

NEROLI DUFFY
MARILYN BARRICK

FOR MORE INFORMATION

Summit University Press books are available at fine bookstores worldwide and at your favorite on-line bookseller.

For a free catalog of our books and products or to learn more about the spiritual techniques featured in this book, please contact:

Summit University Press
PO Box 5000
Corwin Springs, MT 59030-5000 USA
Telephone: 1-800-245-5445 or 406-848-9500
Fax: 1-800-221-8307 or 406-848-9555
www.summituniversitypress.com
info@summituniversitypress.com

ELIZABETH CLARE PROPHET is a world-renowned author. Among her best-sellers are *Fallen Angels and the Origins of Evil, Saint Germain's Prophecy for the New Millennium, The Lost Years of Jesus: Documentary Evidence of Jesus' 17-Year Journey to the East*, and her 10-book series Pocket Guides to Practical Spirituality including *How to Work with Angels, Soul Mates and Twin Flames* and *Alchemy of the Heart*.

She has pioneered techniques in practical spirituality, including the use of the creative power of sound for personal growth and world transformation. Her books are translated into more than 20 languages.

NEROLI DUFFY was trained as a medical doctor in Australia and England and practiced in family medicine and anesthesia for ten years. As a physician and later as a minister, she has worked with many people, especially teenagers, who have faced the issue of suicide. Seeing first-hand the great need for the healing of the soul, she now practices as a minister, writing and lecturing internationally on spirituality and healing and on the Teachings of the Ascended Masters.

MARILYN C. BARRICK, Ph.D., minister, psychologist and transformational therapist, is the author of a seven-book, self-help series on spiritual psychology, a synthesis of her knowledge of sacred text, clinical expertise and life's wisdom. The first five books highlight personal and spiritual growth through understanding the ins and outs of love, change, dreams, emotions and the soul. The remaining two books will focus on children and family and past lives.

In addition to private practice as a clinical psychologist, Dr. Barrick serves as a consultant and conducts seminars and workshops in the U.S.A., Canada and Europe. Visit Dr. Barrick's web site at www.spiritualpsychology.com.